BUYING
AND SELLING
A HOME
IN TODAY'S
MARKET

BUYING AND SELLING A HOME IN TODAY'S MARKET

BY
JOAN MEYERS

A DELL BOOK

Published by
The Kiplinger Washington Editors, Inc.
1729 H Street, N.W.
Washington, D.C. 20006

Distributed by
Dell Publishing Co., Inc.
1 Dag Hammarskjold Plaza
New York, New York 10017

This book is available at a special discount when ordered in
bulk quantities. Contact The Kiplinger Washington Editors,
Inc., at the address above.

Dell ® TM 681510, Dell Publishing Co., Inc.

ISBN: 0-440-03633-X

Printed in the United States of America
First Printing: May 1983
Seventh Printing—April 1985

CONTENTS

PREFACE   *xi*

PART ONE
FOR BUYERS

1 To Buy or Not to Buy   3
Are you ready and able?

Do you *really* want to buy? • Will your
goals change? • The pros and cons of
homeownership

2 Qualifying Yourself as a Buyer   12
Do you have what it takes?

How much cash? • What can you
afford? • Look at your credit the way a
lender does

3 Who Are the Lenders?   22
And how will they size you up?

The sources of money • Price isn't the
only criterion • Commercial banks •
Savings and loan associations •
Mortgage companies

4 Your Choice of Loans   29
Old, new and mixed

Fixed-rate mortgages •
Graduated-payment mortgages •
Adjustable-rate loans • Some common
adjustable-rate mortgages • Other kinds
of mortgages • When the seller is the
lender

5 Planning Your House Hunt   64
Strategy and tactics

Anxiety attacks • Know your needs •
Your must list vs. your want list •
Defining your ideal • Why the "perfect"
home turns sour • Identify your veto
zones • Pinpoint your prejudices •
Decoding the classified ads

6 The Great Housing Flea Market   91
*A home with a past or brand-new, a condo,
a mobile?*

Are you a commuter? • New-house
advantages and disadvantages •
Older-house advantages and
disadvantages • Should you consider
condominiums? • Condominium
advantages and disadvantages • Look at
today's mobile homes, too

7 The Truth About Location   106
Is it really all that important?

Sound location or social address? •
What is "location," anyhow? •
Appraising a neighborhood • Spotting
blight • Picking a future winner •
Avoiding a future loser • Changes from
the outside

8 **Broker, Agent, Realtor**   *120*
Who's who?

The competency question • Finding an
agent • You can also hire a buyer-agent
• What to look for in an agent • How to
pick a broker

9 **You Found It! Should You Grab It?**   *129*
Not until you've sought professional advice

Using a pro • What kind of advice
should you seek? • Evaluate the advice
you get

10 **Wangling the Best Deal for Yourself**   *138*
Know what you want

The psychology of negotiating • Your
offer in writing • What's in the contract?

11 **Getting a Good Title**   *148*
*Without it, your dream home could be a
nightmare*

Buying title insurance • Hazards of a
cloudy title • Common title problems •
To avoid delays • How to take title

12 **Taking the Shocks Out of Settlement**   *170*
This is the last hurdle

The costs you face • Be prepared to
negotiate

13 **Tax Angles of Homeownership**   *178*
You get a break from Uncle Sam

The tax side of buying • The tax side of
owning • The tax side of selling •
Moving expenses count, too

PART TWO

FOR SELLERS

14 Before You Hang That "For Sale" Sign   *203*
Ask yourself: Is this sale necessary?
Keeping your gain • Remodeling could
be a better way to go • Profits are only
part of it • Maybe you need an equity
loan • The cost advantage of staying put

15 Polishing Up the Merchandise   *209*
Once you've decided to sell
Get your place in shape • Sales tricks
that work • Make sure everyone knows
what's for sale • Take a fresh look at
your old haunts

16 Setting the Right Price   *218*
Not too high, not too low
How to get price information • An
objective approach • The price if you're
the lender

17 Do You Want to Be the Lender?   *226*
Watch out for potential pitfalls
Pluses and minuses • Running a credit
check • Make sure the loan can be
insured • Could you sell your paper?

18 Searching for a Broker   *235*
Who is right for you?
Check out the firm • Interview your
former neighbors • What kind of listing?
• The listing agreement

19 Being Your Own Middleman 246
"For Sale by Owner"

Going it alone • Give yourself enough
lead time • Maintain convenient hours •
Don't just show it—*sell* it! • Bringing
them in • Lookers, buyers and selected
clients

20 Negotiating Your Way to a Contract 260
Both sides want a good deal

On your own • Using an agent • When
the contract arrives • Take a hard look
at the buyers • The contract itself

21 Getting Ready for Settlement 272
It should go without a hitch

The papers you'll need • Your seller
costs

GLOSSARY 277

INDEX 287

Preface

If you are on your way to the real estate market to buy or sell a home, you need to be up-to-date on the revolution that has been going on.

The entire real estate industry is recovering from the worst drubbing it has suffered since the Great Depression. Out of this experience have come major changes, some permanent. The biggest change is in the mortgage: who makes it, how much it costs, and how it is repaid.

From the outside looking in, things might not seem that different—"For Sale" signs go up, brokers show houses to clients, "Sold" signs appear, old neighbors move out and new ones move in. Outwardly, it looks like business as usual. Well, it's not the way it used to be.

The affordable home (meaning the affordable mortgage) can be found, but it could be in a different package from the long-familiar conventionally financed deal. It used to be that once you found a home you wanted and could afford, financing it was more or less routine. Often the broker took care of it as one of his services incidental to the sale. Now you have to be sharper and more diligent, whether you are a buyer or a seller.

The old American game of musical chairs—live in a home for a few years and then trade up—has slowed down. It's important now to make a good choice because you may be living in the home longer than you think—which is all the more reason to find a mortgage you can live with through thick and thin.

If you are a buyer, you will need to shop for a mortgage as intensively as you shop for the home itself. There are many that seem affordable but could turn out to be disastrous for you. You need a strong grasp of the details to avoid the ones capable of delivering a lethal shock to your budget.

If you are a seller, there is a buyer out there for the house you are offering, but it will take more than a "For Sale" sign in your front yard to land him.

This book is divided into two parts. Part I is for buyers, Part II for sellers. Whichever you are, it won't hurt to skim the part addressed to the other fellow. You'll gain an insight into what concerns the major players in the game of buying and selling a home, and that information could help you make a better deal.

The book was written by Joan Meyers, who has many years of experience in the real estate business, beginning with her first license as an agent with her father's brokerage firm in Lansing, Mich. She sold real estate while attending Michigan State University's School of Journalism and after graduating she worked in Washington, D.C., reporting on housing and other subjects for UPI, the *Journal of Commerce*, the Bureau of National Affairs and the Research Institute of America. She also operated her own real estate brokerage company in Washington before moving to Phoenix. She now divides her time among writing, conducting seminars and counseling in real estate.

Several members of the editorial staff of *Changing Times* magazine also helped prepare this book. Special recognition should go to Research Associate Priscilla Gichuru, who put in long days and many weekends gathering and verifying information, and to Kevin McCormally, who contributed the chapter on the tax aspects of homeownership.

I hope this book will steer you through the rough waters of home buying and selling, whether you are a neophyte or an experienced buyer coming back for updating on some of the fast-paced changes that are taking place in the 1980s.

AUSTIN H. KIPLINGER

PART ONE

FOR BUYERS

1

To Buy or Not to Buy

Are you ready and able?

With real estate prices still high and no significant declines in sight, you may have to accept a mortgage with payments that will rise as fast as your income. Is buying a home still a good bet under those conditions?

• *Not if you are a renter at heart and just want to pick up a quick profit.*
• *Not if your chief reason for buying a home is to beat rising rents by freezing your housing costs in the form of a stable mortgage payment.*

But the answer is yes if what appeal to you are the traditional reasons for homeownership: to have a sense of security, to build an estate, to put down roots, to have room to spread out and freedom to indulge your own tastes and hobbies, to establish yourself in the community, to benefit from the tax deductibility of all that interest and to create an enforced savings program.

The one thing that has become somewhat tarnished in that time-honored list of homeowning benefits is the sense of security. In recent years some homeowners have found themselves strapped to keep up the mortgage payments, and for them homeowning has become more a burden than a support.

For buyers and renters alike, housing now takes a bigger bite proportionately out of monthly income than it did before the price runup of the late 1970s. Rents may lag six months to a year, but they always catch up. If the bite gets too severe, the renter can lower his housing costs by moving to a cheaper rental unit. Once you've bought a house, however, you are committed.

Today's prices can mean either a bigger stretch in the family budget or less house. With many of the new mortgages, housing costs can also mean that you're not so likely to get ahead of the game as you were when you could expect your income to rise regularly and your mortgage payment to remain the same. Now the only way many people can buy is to pledge themselves to a program that means the payments will rise with their income.

Despite those disadvantages, however, the drive for homeownership remains strong. The questions you must resolve for yourself: Will a home purchase add to your sense of well-being? Or will the payments be so burdensome that there's no money left for anything else?

To arrive at the answers, you must:

• Analyze your financial picture.

• Get advice from a lender about how much mortgage you can carry.
• Match that figure to the market to learn what you can buy.

You should know before you start that you are probably going to have to make some compromises. Even when interest rates got up to 18% and 19%, mortgage lenders remained busy—not making many loans, to be sure, but taking applications from people who were *trying* to qualify no matter what. Many Americans appear willing to compromise their dream of homeownership by taking a smaller or older home, but they are not willing to give it up altogether.

DO YOU *REALLY* WANT TO BUY?

Before you even look into the affordability question, give some thought to the disadvantages of homeownership. Why take on the responsibility for those relentless mortgage payments, knowing full well that the lender isn't going to be understanding if you miss payments because you blew your budget on a trip to Europe or a sporty new car?

Why give up weekends to enlist with other long-suffering householders in the war against crabgrass? Or if your home is to be an apartment, why let yourself in for those tedious owners' meetings, which are the crabgrass of condominium living?

Why not become a permanent renter and invest in something else?

The real estate shake-out of the early 1980s has changed the focus of home buying. There is much less competition from the inflation fighters who grabbed a second, third or even fourth house or condo as an inflation hedge and thereby drove prices even higher. They have withdrawn now that real estate is no longer the speculator's delight that it was in the late '70s.

Today's potential home buyer is more likely to ask, "Should I buy something I'll enjoy living in, or is it better just to keep on renting?" That is not to say that a home isn't still a good investment. But making money on a home is no longer a major motivation for buying one.

A home is usually a safe place to put your money, but if you are looking for a quick turnover, home buying is not your game. On the other hand, a home retains its appeal as the only investment you can live in.

What makes the buy vs. rent debate difficult is that you can't come to firm conclusions. Even with most variable mortgages, you can project a worst-case scenario for your monthly housing cost when you buy. Not so with renting. When you decide to become a permanent renter, you are gambling that through good times and bad there will be an ample supply of rental units with comparable amenities at prices more economical than the monthly cost of buying. That gamble is riskier now that small investors have become disenchanted with playing landlord for houses in which the rents don't cover expenses and rising property values can't be counted on for fast profits. Big investors prefer the more profitable commercial investments over residential.

One long-range trend does appear clear: If you remain a renter, your chances of doing so are much less in a single-family unit than in a multiunit building because the economics are against single-family rental residences as investments.

WILL YOUR GOALS CHANGE?

Psychologists rank buying a home high on the list of stress-producing events, not just because it is the biggest purchase most people make in a lifetime but because it forces you to look at all kinds of questions involving goals, commitment and life-style. All of these should be up for review when you are purchasing a home. Difficult as this exercise is, omitting it is folly.

To rush into the market without such preparation is to join that horde of buyers who charge out, with or without an armload of facts and figures, searching for answers without knowing the real questions. They search for weeks or months through all sorts of property, ending up awash in facts, figures and reports and feeling frustrated and confused because they have no focus for their investigation. Such a search ends in one of two ways, either of which is a kind of defeat: They quit, or they buy anything just to get the agony over with.

You can spare yourself all that by asking yourself the sorts of questions an experienced real estate counselor would ask you. The role of the real estate counselor is a common one in large commercial real estate deals. These professionals specialize in giving advice instead of selling property. Because their judgment is valued, they are paid on a fee basis instead of on a commission. From them the investor, particularly the out-of-town investor, feels he can get more disinterested advice than he could from an agent who has a commission riding on the sale. The counselor's advice may be "don't buy property X" or "don't buy that sort of property this year," advice a buyer is not likely to hear from an agent about his own listing.

Unfortunately, there is not enough money in residential counseling for really qualified professionals to engage in it exclusively. If there were, a counselor might draw you out on your attitude about owning a home. Are you really the home-buying type? What do you want *in* a home and what do you want *from* a home: security? shelter? image? Is home buying an incidental part or the major part of your investment program? What are your fixed requirements? What are your points of flexibility?

The next chapter will help you counsel yourself so you can do well with your home purchase even with a half-trained or indifferent agent. Any agent can steer you toward the right price range, but only analysis of what you want in a home will steer you to the right place.

Contrast this value-setting, priority-establishing approach with the one you are likely to experience at the hands of some agents. You walk in cold off the street into a real estate office, where an agent asks you your name, address, home and work phone, how much money you can pay down and how many bedrooms you require. Before you know it, you are being whisked off in an automobile and whammo! You are deep into the shopping routine.

This is the mindless way many house hunts start, and this is why so many of them end in disappointment. If the first trip out proves fruitless, you start with another agent, then another and another until your patience is exhausted or you luck into something.

The reason that so many purchasers and agents don't communicate well is that many agents assume that because the buyer has presented himself, he is ready. The agent takes literally whatever the buyer blurts out as his requirements. Some agents don't know how or don't take the time to counsel a buyer.

An experienced and intuitive agent senses when the real questions haven't been grappled with and helps the client through the process. If you find such an agent, stick with him. (Incidentally, many agents, home buyers and sellers are women, but for convenience, we'll use the masculine pronouns throughout this book.) A good agent won't let the buyer go for a test drive until he has determined what the appropriate model is. If you don't come to some conclusions about what living style you want and whether buying a house will help or cripple your savings and investment program, all the looking is useless.

THE PROS AND CONS OF HOMEOWNERSHIP

It cannot be said too often or too emphatically: *Buying a home is not a pure investment.* Treating it as though it were produces a bundle of facts and figures but falls far short of giving you the perspective you need to make your big decision.

There are a number of benefits, not all of them financial, that go with owning a home, and there are a number of burdens, only some of which are financial, that also go with it. You have to decide whether the trade-offs are worth it to you.

Financial arguments FOR homeownership

• A home is a relatively safe place to invest.

• Through the mortgage you enroll in a regular, enforced savings program.

• You have a reasonable hope of controlling—or at least predicting—your housing costs.

• The home is a possible springboard to a better home later.

• The mortgage interest and real estate taxes are tax-deductible.

• You can defer taxes on the profit if you sell and reinvest in another home within 24 months.

• Profits up to $125,000 are tax-free—*without* reinvesting—if you are age 55 or older when you sell.

Financial arguments AGAINST homeownership

• Your cash is tied up. (This disadvantage is now reduced with the new loans on equity discussed in Chapter 14.)

• You face unpredictable cash outlays for expensive replacements (the roof or furnace, for instance), plus regular repairs and maintenance.

• Depending on the size of the mortgage payment, it may be hard to maintain your savings and investment programs for vacations, college tuition and other things.

• You might be forced to sell in a down market.

• The mortgage payments could escalate uncontrollably if you have a no-ceiling adjustable loan.

• If you have a balloon-payment arrangement, it could come due before you have enough equity to refinance or when money is either very expensive or hard to find.

2

Qualifying Yourself as a Buyer

Do you have what it takes?

Once you become a serious home shopper, you should review your financial situation to determine what you can pay down and what you can carry monthly.

How much cash you have in the bank and how much rent you now pay are clues, but only clues. The earlier you know not only what you can easily handle but also the maximum stretch that's available to you, the better. It's a rare buyer who hasn't wanted a home a notch or two above his price level. That makes him vulnerable to the exhortations of the eager agent to "dig a little deeper."

Before you start looking, you ought to know absolutely what your comfort zone is, what is possible with some stretch, and what is out of the question. Not many buyers start off that well prepared, which accounts for much of the frustration associated with the home search.

The worksheets provided in this chapter call for the same type of information a lender will want from you when you seek a loan. At this stage you need to set an upper limit on the down payment and an upper limit on the monthly payment. Then you will have to visit a lender to get those figures translated into the several kinds of mortgages available and, consequently, into a price.

Besides preparing you for the lender, this exercise will prevent you from making the kind of mistake that happens every day when home shoppers rush into the market and find a "dream" house only to learn that they are $5,000 or $10,000 short on cash or too light in income to qualify for the necessary mortgage.

HOW MUCH CASH?

For many people—especially first-time buyers— the most sensible answer these days to how much cash you need for a home purchase almost always is "all you can afford."

When interest rates were cheaper, it often made sense to use as little of your own money and as much of the lender's as possible. Now that lenders can pass unforeseen changes in the cost of money on to the borrower in variable-rate loans, it probably behooves you to borrow as little as possible.

In the lower price ranges you may be able to buy with 5% down if the home is eligible for an FHA loan or the builder is subsidizing the rates. Qualified veterans don't have to pay anything down on a home approved for a VA loan.

When neither FHA nor VA financing is involved, the common down payment for a new mortgage from a commercial lender is 20%. It is frequently less in deals in which the seller takes back paper—that is, finances part of the deal himself.

There is always the temptation to put down as little as possible. You should hold back some cash for new furniture, draperies and other household items, and more if you are buying an older house in which the plumbing or the roof might spring a leak. But don't keep the cash investment down simply because the seller or lender is agreeable to it.

The more cash you pay down, the less you will have to pay monthly on the mortgage.

You don't have to have the cash in the bank when you start your deal provided it is in assets that can be readily sold, such as stocks or bonds. If your money is tied up in such illiquid assets as other real estate, give yourself plenty of time to either sell them or borrow on them.

If you don't have a recent net worth statement, this is the time to put one together. The particular usefulness of the net worth statement is that by inventorying your assets, you can determine the maximum down payment you can make with safety. You will need it later when you talk to a lender anyway.

Home-buying time is the time to gather whatever you have scattered about in the way of assets that by themselves may not amount to much or that you might be tempted to cash in at some later time and spend the proceeds for some luxury or other. Do you have such illiquid collectibles as coins, art glass, antiques, or perhaps something you inherited, such as a vacant lot at the lake, jewelry or securities that have not been performing particularly well? Consider converting them to home equity. They may have a better chance of growth in a home than in their present form.

Equally important to a review of your assets is a review of your current liabilities. With an up-to-date listing of your assets minus your liabilities, both you and your potential lender will know your current net worth and have a picture of your financial readiness to buy. A separate analysis of your monthly budget will indicate how much mortgage payment you can carry each month.

Here's a worksheet for inventorying your net worth.

FIGURING YOUR NET WORTH

ASSETS

cash available (savings and checking
   accounts)   _____

investments (current value of stocks,
   bonds, mutual funds)   _____

certificates of deposit   _____

accounts receivable (money owed to you)   _____

real estate (appraised value)   _____

automobiles (resale value)   _____

personal property (current value of
furniture, jewelry, sound system, art,
antiques, collectibles, professional
equipment) _____

insurance (cash value) _____

annuities (surrender value) _____

other assets _____

   TOTAL ASSETS _____

LIABILITIES

debts to banks and other commercial
lenders _____

real estate mortgages (balance due) _____

personal debts (to private individuals) _____

charge account bills _____

unpaid income taxes _____

auto loan _____

other debts _____

   TOTAL LIABILITIES _____

NET WORTH (assets minus liabilities) $ _____

WHAT CAN YOU AFFORD?

What counts heavily in determining the payment you can carry is not just how much you earn but how much you have left to spend.

The biggest favor you can do yourself in getting ready to buy a home is to get rid of as many monthly debts as you can. Lenders won't permit you to borrow part of your down payment, but if you have a friend or relative who will pay off your installment loans, you will qualify for a larger loan. A big car payment can reduce your borrowing capability by as much as $10,000 because it cuts deeply into what a lender will approve for you in a monthly payment. If you are planning the purchase of a new car or new furniture, postpone it until after you've bought your home. You may think you can carry both, but a lender might not.

The lender will scrutinize your monthly income and outgo at the time you apply for a loan. He won't try to play fortune teller and guess how much you may be carrying in payments after you get the loan.

The less you pay down, the more closely your finances will be examined. What's left after deductions of all kinds and after you've paid your recurring monthly obligations becomes extremely important.

Rules vary for conventional, FHA and VA loans. In the case of the government-backed loans, the lender will want to know how many people you are supporting and their ages. The reason for this is that government rules require the lender to estimate your living costs rather than take your word for it. The theory is that buyers who don't have enough left to live on may eventually default.

How much the lender is willing to look the other way if your income is a little light or how much weight he is willing to give to your paid-for possessions depends greatly on whether he is planning to hold your mortgage in his own portfolio or sell it to an investor. Interpretations vary from area to area. The rule is shop, shop, shop!

Here is a worksheet for figuring how much you have available monthly for mortgage payments:

HOW MUCH CAN YOU PAY MONTHLY?

I. Family income

annual salaries (before deductions) _____

bonuses, commissions _____

interest, dividends _____

other _____

total annual income _____

monthly income (divide annual total by 12) _____

II. Family expenses other than housing costs

food _____

clothing _____

debt payments _____

alimony or child-support payments _____

education _____

home furnishings _____

life, health, auto insurance _____

recreation _____

transportation _____

medical _____

charities, other contributions _____

taxes, social security, pension contributions _____

other _____

amount you would like to save _____

total annual expenses _____

monthly expenses (divide annual total by 12) _____

III. Housing budget

monthly income, from Section I _____

monthly expenses, from Section II _____

maximum amount available for housing
(subtract expenses from income) _____

LOOK AT YOUR CREDIT THE WAY
A LENDER DOES

If you have a question about whether anything in your credit record may present a problem in getting a loan, you would be wise to check on it before making the application.

Federal law gives you the right to look at your own credit report. You can't get the information by telephone unless you have made a written request to do so, but by going in person to your local credit reporting agency, presenting positive identification and paying a small fee, you can read what will be reported about you. If there are several credit reporting agencies in your city, ask a few of the bigger lenders which one they use for residential loan credit review. The efficiency of the reporting systems varies greatly, which is why lenders prefer some credit reporters over others.

A lender looks for these red flags: chronic late payments, overextension (a regular pattern of buying a number of big-ticket items at the same time), garnishments and, the biggest flag of all, bankruptcy.

If you have in your file an unfavorable report turned in by a creditor with whom you had a dispute, now is the time to call on him and arrive at some kind of peace. You may decide it's better to swallow some pride and make a settlement. Your record may still contain information on the case, but a lender is likely to view it more favorably if you have taken care of it when you apply for a loan. If you feel you have been unfairly tagged for nonpayment or slow payment, you should write a well-documented letter setting forth your understanding of the facts and file it with the credit bureau.

Any old credit skeletons probably won't be on the record. Lenders look most sharply at your credit performance for the three years immediately preceding your application.

Your employment record will also be looked at. Longevity on the job or in the same line of work is a big plus. Job hopping is viewed with extreme caution by lenders unless there is evidence of a steady increase in income with each change.

3

Who Are the Lenders?

And how will they size you up?

After you have done your budget calculations on what you can afford to carry each month, your next step should be to talk to a lender. Don't accept a real estate agent's calculations for what size loan you can carry unless you are convinced that your figures will be submitted to a lender. When there were only fixed-rate mortgages to contend with, experienced agents could pinpoint your buying capacity fairly accurately. With today's more complex plans, the agent is likely to want to put you in touch with a lender who does a thorough prequalifying interview.

Only a professional loan officer can translate your monthly figure into a price range. In a mortgage market where one lender can talk to you about dozens of ways to buy a home, you can see that professional interpretation is a must.

In this prequalifying procedure you exchange your net worth and monthly payment information with a lender for a thorough work-up of all the loans you might qualify for. Not until you have this in hand are you ready to start looking for a home. The service is offered free by the more aggressive lenders because they find it pays off for them as well as their customers. From it the lenders get a number of loan applications—solid ones, since the customers have been screened.

Prequalifying can save you endless fumbling in the market. It will save you the disappointment of picking a home only to find at the end of a long, tedious shopping and negotiating process that you can't swing the loan. It can also save you the frustration of learning too late that you could have carried a more expensive home than you thought.

No longer is figuring your price range a simple process of coming up with a monthly figure and translating it into a price with the help of an amortization table. Adjustable loans confuse the issue. The same monthly payment can buy you a home in several price ranges, depending on the kind of mortgage you take out. Though some of these new loans can be treacherous if they have no limit, or cap, others afford you the opportunity to buy more house than you could with the traditional fixed-rate loan. You need a professional loan officer to lay all this out for you.

The lender who does the prequalifying doesn't have to be the one you use when you actually take a loan. When you're ready to do that, you should talk to more than one lender.

THE SOURCES OF MONEY

You might obtain your mortgage from any one of four major sources of mortgage funds:

• The owner (seller) from whom you are buying the home.
• A savings and loan.
• A commercial bank.
• A mortgage company.

Seller financing characteristically is a little cheaper than a loan from a savings and loan, bank or mortgage company, but it has its hazards. This kind of "creative financing" is a creature of a market in which commercial loans are unaffordable or even unavailable. When interest rates fall, sellers pull back on playing lender. The pros and cons of various types of creative financing are discussed in the next chapter.

Which of the commercial lenders offers the best loan changes from month to month and from locale to locale. The fortunes of these lenders rise and fall with their ability to sell your loan to investors in the national mortgage market. The condition of that market depends on the supply and, consequently, the price of money. The mortgage lender is a gambler: He gambles that he can lend money to you at retail rates higher than the wholesale rate at which he borrows. If he wins, he prospers, as savings and loan associations did for decades. If he gets caught with old loans made at cheap rates and has to borrow new money at high rates, he could go under.

There is no guaranteed source of mortgage funds. Lenders have regular outlets for large packages of loans, but not always at the price they would like to receive. Large purchasers of mortgages tell the lenders what *they* will pay, not the other way around. So it's a volatile business, and the lender who is fat in October may be lean in May. You have to keep checking to find one who has money to lend.

There are two kinds of costs to every loan: the *interest* (which is the rent on the money you pay for the life of the loan) and the *points* (which are a one-time charge up front). A point equals 1% of the amount of the loan. If you're offered an $80,000 loan at 12% with 8 points, you have to pay $8,000 to get the loan and you have to pay 12% interest on the $80,000. These two price factors are susceptible to frequent change. If your house hunt stretches over a period of months in a rapidly changing market, it is possible for the interest rate to change several times.

What the lender charges you depends not only on how much he has to pay for his money but also on how much local competition he faces from other mortgage lenders. The competitive factor can alter the price of loans because aggressive lenders will cut their profit margins if they have to.

Generally speaking, a large lender can borrow more advantageously than a small one. Loans in little batches are more expensive than multimillion- and billion-dollar packages of mortgages. That doesn't mean a big lender's loan to you will be cheaper. What it does mean frequently is that the large lender has funds to lend when the small ones do not. The large lender may also be able to offer a greater variety of new-style loans.

PRICE ISN'T THE ONLY CRITERION

There are literally dozens of ways to finance a home purchase. Some plans enable you to shift much of the burden to the future. Others are more expensive to get into but offer you a guaranteed rate. Another might enable you to buy a more expensive house than any of the others.

Try to find a lender who can offer you a variety of financing plans. Lenders differ widely in how helpful they are in their eagerness to understand your housing objectives and to tailor a loan to meet them. Like real estate agents, some loan officers are routine order takers and some are problem solvers.

When loan shopping, it's wise to check at least one lender in every major type: savings and loans, banks and mortgage companies.

COMMERCIAL BANKS

Try your own bank, but don't be discouraged if you get turned down. Mortgage loans aren't favorites with commercial bankers. They much prefer short-term business loans and smaller consumer loans, such as car financing. However, commercial banks have become a little more interested in mortgages since flexible rates and shorter-term loans came into vogue. Your bank may not be your best source, but it is a possibility that should be checked, particularly since it already knows you. Don't leave your banker without getting a suggestion for where else you should try.

SAVINGS AND LOAN ASSOCIATIONS

Try several. They differ greatly in financial health and in their approach to lending. Don't assume that because one s&l doesn't have any money, or doesn't have a program that seems attractive to you, the others won't. Whether a particular s&l has an interesting mortgage for you depends on how aggressively it has moved into offering the new products made possible by deregulation, such as money-market accounts. S&l's have always been a major source of home mortgages, but deregulation, aggressive lending by mortgage bankers, creative financing and the housing slump have combined to reduce their share of the market.

A change in s&l operation is another factor in the availability of s&l mortgage funds. Increasingly, the associations, like other lenders, are selling their loans to a secondary market, enabling them to replenish their supply of lendable funds.

MORTGAGE COMPANIES

The mortgage bankers may not be as physically conspicuous in your town as the s&l with its many branch offices, but you should look for them. One's office may be prominent, with a staff of 20 to 30 people; another's may be a two-person office tucked away in a shopping center. Either setup may have access to a billion-dollar source of funds. Ask both your real estate broker and your agent which mortgage bankers are currently lending. (Often the broker is closer to the lending scene than the agent.) You might also ask the escrow officers in a title company. Check the Yellow Pages under "Mortgages."

The home office of the mortgage company may be in New York, Dallas, San Francisco or Detroit, but its presence in your city will be represented by a loan correspondent with the authority to approve a loan.

Mortgage bankers as a group have been very active in alternative financing. You are likely to be offered more kinds of plans by a mortgage banker than by other kinds of lenders. What's unique about the mortgage banker is his specialization. He is the only one whose sole activity is the making of mortgages. Mortgage bankers have increased their market share from a mere 19% in the banner real estate year of 1978 to 31% in the depressed real estate market of mid-1982.

There are likely to be several mortgage bankers in your city. Before deciding on anything, you should talk to more than one. Mortgage banking is a keenly competitive business.

4

Your Choice of Loans

Old, new and mixed

FIXED-RATE MORTGAGES

The mortgage with a fixed rate and fixed term is the kind most people are most familiar with and one with no surprises in it. It is the traditional 30-year (or 25-year or 20-year) loan that doesn't change from the day you get it: one interest rate, one payment rate and a steadily declining balance. Most of the more than one trillion dollars' worth of outstanding home mortgage debt in America is in fixed-rate mortgages.

Mortgage lenders expect the fixed-rate loan to survive but to continue to cost more than some of the newer types of flexible loans. To make it less risky, the lender usually wants both a higher interest rate and more points. There will always be some lenders who like locking up interest rates for a long time, but the 30-year, fixed-rate loan may not be the best bargain for you.

Advantages. Certainty is the big plus. You know exactly how much you will be paying for principal and interest, so you know your loan payments won't change.

Disadvantages. Both the interest rate and the points may be higher than for some of the newer types of loans. That means your income must be higher to qualify than it would need to be for a loan that calls for lower payments in the beginning.

You probably shouldn't count on refinancing a fixed-rate mortgage if interest rates should drop. They would have to go down several percentage points before refinancing would be worthwhile. Prepayment penalties and other costs usually make refinancing impractical unless you have substantial appreciation in the house.

Most new fixed-rate conventional loans are not assumable by someone else at the same rate because they carry due-on-sale clauses. Such a clause and a prepayment penalty can be important obstacles when you want to sell.

GRADUATED-PAYMENT MORTGAGES

These are fixed-rate loans for which the monthly payments in the early years are deliberately set lower than the amortization schedule requires. As years go by, the payments are gradually increased according to a formula set by the lender and agreed to by the borrower.

The initial payments on a GPM are not enough to cover fully the interest due on the loan. The difference is added to the loan balance, and future interest payments are calculated on the higher loan balance, meaning that later payments must be higher than they otherwise would have been in order to pay off the loan. Normally, payments are structured to rise for a set period, often five or ten years, after which they remain constant for the remainder of the payback period.

A GPM may be a conventional, VA or FHA mortgage.

Advantages. Because payments are lower in the early years, GPMs can make a home affordable to buyers whose incomes may be relatively low now but can be expected to increase steadily in the future.

Disadvantages. The interest that you don't pay in the early years of the loan serves to increase your indebtedness. If you sell after only a few years, you could wind up owing more on the home than you borrowed in the first place. Your gamble that appreciation in the value of the house will offset your increased indebtedness may or may not work out.

If you hold on to the home for the life of the mortgage, you'll have to pay back the interest you borrowed in the early years, meaning the mortgage will be more expensive in the long run than a fixed-rate loan at the same interest rate without the graduated payment feature.

ADJUSTABLE-RATE LOANS

Some adjustable loans are better than others. Uniformity does not exist yet, and may never to the extent it used to. In the meantime there are many different kinds of adjustable loans available and your choices vary from lender to lender.

Lenders speak a language all their own. It's a mistake for you to try to talk their lingo. The two of you could be using a simple word in entirely different ways. Or you could be using an acronym like ARM, which stands for adjustable-rate mortgage, and have an understanding of it far different from your lender's, since each lender can have his own ARM.

To avoid these pitfalls, it's best to *describe* the loan you want as you go from lender to lender rather than try to *name* it. Despite all the variations on these loans, they have certain common elements. The lender wants protection against rising interest rates and hopes to pass that risk on to the borrower. He is offering a number of features that he hopes are attractive enough to make borrowers willing to pick up that burden.

By looking at certain basic elements, it is possible to compare one adjustable-rate mortgage with another and an adjustable-rate with a fixed-rate mortgage. The two most important basic elements to scrutinize:

• What protection you'd get against unpredictably high payments.
• How adjustments would be handled.

With an adjustable-rate loan the best protection is a cap on the interest rate. With a graduated-payment loan the best protection is a fixed schedule of payments.

The lender will be asking you all kinds of questions to qualify you as a borrower. It's up to you to ask the lender a number of pointed questions to qualify his adjustable loan as a debt you're willing to take on. To make sure you are getting what you think you are getting, press the lender for answers to the following questions:

- On what index or interest rate are changes in payments based?
- Can the lender change the index during the course of the loan?
- What is the term of the loan?
- Does the loan have a cap? What is it?
- Is the cap on the payment or on the interest rate?
- Is the cap for a few years only or for the life of the loan?
- Is there a cap on how much the payment can rise in any one year?
- Is there a limit on how much the monthly payment can decrease in case of declining interest rates?
- How often is the payment adjusted?
- What's the maximum monthly payment?
- Does the loan call for negative amortization (meaning the amount due increases because the interest owed exceeds the monthly payment)? If so, what is the cap on the negative amortization and what is the effect of that cap?
- How much *more* than a fixed-rate loan could this loan cost in total interest paid?
- Can you refinance the loan or accelerate payments without penalty?

If the loan has no cap, you would have no protection against soaring payments.

Whether the cap is on the payment or the interest rate is important, as you'll see in the following discussion of various kinds of adjustable loans.

If the cap is on the payment, the typical loan contract allows negative amortization if rising interest rates would require payments higher than the cap. The amount of interest owed that's not covered by your payment would be added to the loan balance for a certain period or within a certain limit. After that, payments would be adjusted to fully amortize the loan over the remaining term at the then-current interest rate. This kind of cap controls your initial payments but can raise the total cost of the loan.

If the cap is on the interest rate, your loan will not go into negative amortization. Instead, as interest rates rise, the payments will increase to whatever is necessary to amortize the loan. If you can afford it, this loan is much better than one that caps the payment because it controls your total interest cost. You could be making higher future payments, but the cap on how much the interest rate can rise allows you to determine in advance what your worst-case payments might be.

Some caps are temporary, perhaps covering only the first five years of the loan. A permanent cap is much better. Without permanence all you accomplish is postponement of the possibility of very high payments.

When rates are rising, the ideal adjustable-rate loan is one with the lowest possible cap on the interest rate and the least frequent adjustments.

Loans tied to a monthly index can keep you in a constant state of change and unpredictability if the interest rate market turns volatile. One to three years is usually a manageable period for adjustments; five years is better if you can get it.

The kinds of indexes used for adjustable loans may change from time to time. Lenders, needless to say, want the index that is most sensitive to changes in the cost of money.

If you're considering an adjustable-rate loan, look for one tied to a longer-term index. A mortgage tied to three-year Treasury securities, for example, will give you more stable monthly payments than one tied to six-month Treasury bills.

Can you refinance without penalty? The answer varies from loan to loan and from lender to lender. In general, you are more likely to be able to change an adjustable-rate loan without penalty than you are a fixed-rate loan. The same is true of assumability. (VA and FHA loans are assumable, whether adjustable or fixed-rate.)

If interest rates go down and seem likely to stay down, you might want to refinance with a cheaper loan if you have a plan with locked-in payment increases.

SOME COMMON ADJUSTABLE-RATE MORTGAGES

ARM WITHOUT A CAP. The adjustable-rate mortgage, known to federal s&l's as an adjustable mortgage loan (AML), was the first in the spate of inventions made by mortgage lenders in their struggle to find some way to cope with the interest rate crisis.

The hazard of many of these early plans was that they provided no ceiling on payments or interest rates, so they allowed too much volatility at the expense of the borrower. With any ARM or AML—capped or not—your interest rate is tied to an index not under the control of the lender. It could be the rate being paid on six-month U.S. Treasury bills, the yield on five-year Treasury securities or the Federal Home Loan Bank Board index of average mortgage contract rates.

These uncapped loans have prompted the most unfavorable comments about adjustable-rate loans. There were so many horror stories about buyers unable to meet shocking new payments when interest rates soared that some critics suggested that ARMs without caps be outlawed. When interest rates eased downward in 1982, there was less talk about such action.

ARM OR AML WITH A CAP. There is considerably more safety for the borrower here. It's not that these loans are cheaper; they're just safer. There are literally dozens of variations.

Here are two common arrangements:

• Adjustments in interest rates and monthly payments are allowed every five years. Changes are tied to rates for five-year Treasury securities. Although this ARM does not have a cap on interest or payments, its long adjustment period gives the borrower a fixed rate for five years.

• Payments change every three years, but the interest rate is adjusted every six months. A change in payment required by a rise in rates within this three-year interval is added to the balance of the mortgage, creating negative amortization. The interest-rate changes are tied to changes in the rate for six-month U.S. Treasury bills.

GPARM OR GPAML. These are graduated-payment mortgages with an adjustable-rate feature.

The difference between a GPARM and a straight ARM is that in the beginning, payments on a GPARM are insufficient to amortize the loan. To compensate, the payments rise according to a fixed schedule. You know exactly when and by how much for the first several years.

Under a popular version of the GPARM, payments rise at the rate of $7\frac{1}{2}\%$ annually for five years, during which the unpaid portion of the interest is deferred and added to the loan balance. Every five years payments are adjusted to fully amortize the loan balance at the then-current market rate, based on the movement of five-year U.S. Treasury securities.

Advantages. The lower fixed payments make GPARMs easier to qualify for than fixed-rate loans. For some buyers this feature could make the difference in being able to buy a $60,000 home with a graduated-payment mortgage instead of a $50,000 home with a fixed-rate mortgage. For many buyers whose income doesn't qualify them for a fixed-rate loan, it could mean the difference between being able to buy a home and not being able to.

Disadvantages. Your housing costs could rise substantially. There may be no cap or ceiling after the first ten years. If interest rates then go up, no matter how high, you'll have to pay. If interest rates go down while you're locked into the fixed schedule of payment increases, you could be paying at a higher-than-market rate. Some loan contracts limit downward adjustments in interest rates.

The other potential drawbacks to GPARMs are the same as for GPMs, discussed earlier. Also, people on fixed incomes may have difficulty getting GPARMs.

Negative amortization makes the loan easier to carry in the early years, but unless interest rates fall dramatically during that period, such a mortgage might be very expensive if you had to sell in the first few years of ownership, since at that point you might owe more than you borrowed.

OTHER KINDS OF MORTGAGES

THE REFINANCE BLEND. These plans take the place of the straight assumption of an existing loan. Many lenders won't permit you to take over the old loan with the old interest rate. They might, however, make you a better deal than you would get with a completely new fixed-rate loan. The refinance blend is attractive only when market interest rates are high relative to the rate on the property's existing mortgage. When market rates are lower than or equal to the rate on the existing mortgage, there is no incentive to apply for a blended rate.

The deal works like this: The lender takes the old rate for the outstanding balance, applies an agreed-upon rate to the new money you are borrowing and blends the two rates into a single loan.

Say you want to buy a house priced at $80,000. You have $20,000 for a down payment. The seller is carrying a 10% mortgage on which he owes $40,000. The going market rate at the time you want to buy is 13%. The holder of the seller's mortgage might arrange a blended-rate loan for you by allowing you to take over responsibility for the old mortgage and lending you an additional $20,000 at an above-market rate, 14%. But instead of offering you two separate loans, he blends the two amounts into a single mortgage of $60,000 at 12%. Thus, you get a mortgage at below-market rates and the lender gets rid of an old loan that was earning him only 10%.

Advantages. This loan gives you the best of both worlds: a fixed rate with no surprises and an interest rate that is below the market rate.

Disadvantages. There are none created by the blending itself, but since this is usually a standard fixed-rate loan, it shares the fixed rate's disadvantages: Your new blended rate is probably not assumable and there is probably a prepayment penalty if you refinance early in the life of the loan. For a good blend it is important to get a young loan. The more new money you have to add, the less advantageous the blended rate will be.

The chief difficulty with a good blend is finding one.

A home has to have a mortgage with a relatively high balance and relatively low interest rate to make for a good blend. And not every existing loan is a candidate. Ask the lender—or whoever is servicing the old loan—whether FNMA owns the mortgage. If so, you may be able to get a blended mortgage with a rate that's 2 or 3 points below the current market figure. FNMA is so eager to get older loans with cheap rates off its books that it's doing everything possible to facilitate this kind of refinancing—including blending adjustable-rate and graduated-payment loans.

Some other mortgage holders, such as s&l's, will give you a blended rate. You have to ask the company that owns the loan. Or you can ask a mortgage broker or loan officer to find out for you.

THE PERMANENT BUY-DOWN. The permanent buy-down is a scheme for lowering the interest rate for the life of the loan. The builder or other seller pays the lender a lump sum at the time the loan is made in exchange for a lower rate to the buyer. Any kind of loan can be bought down.

Advantages. In addition to whatever pluses attend the basic loan to which the buy-down is applied, there is the added advantage of a permanently lower interest rate.

Disadvantages. On the minus side are the same negatives as the basic loan on which it is based. Sometimes another disadvantage is a much higher price for the home because the seller adds the cost of the buy-down to the price. If you are offered a permanent buy-down, you should shop competitive properties to see how much of a premium you may be paying (or how much of a bargain you may be getting). Some hard-pressed builders take part of their cost out of their profit. A few very hard-pressed ones take it all. More often, though, the cost of the buy-down shows up in the price.

THE TEMPORARY BUY-DOWN. On these, the buy-down period is usually one to three years, but it can be longer. There is no limit on the amount a home buyer or seller can contribute. Anybody can buy down your loan, on either a permanent or a temporary basis: your seller, your builder, your parents, yourself.

A temporary buy-down can be applied to most fixed-rate and certain adjustable-rate mortgages. Temporary buy-downs are not permitted on VA or most FHA graduated-payment mortgages.

Typically, a limited buy-down of a fixed-rate conventional mortgage might reduce the contract interest rate by 3 percentage points the first year, 2 in the second year and 1 in the third. After that, payments would be based on the original interest rate for the remaining years of the loan.

SHARED-APPRECIATION MORTGAGE. In a SAM your lender gives you a big interest break—perhaps 3 or 4 percentage points below the market. In return he gets a portion of the anticipated profit from the eventual sale or refinancing of the home at a prearranged time. The contract between the lender and the borrower will determine how profit is to be measured; it is often based on an appraisal or the sales price if the house is sold at the prearranged time. There may be restrictions on how long you can hold the mortgage or an agreement on when you must sell or refinance.

Advantgages. This is one way to buy a home when you can't do it any other way. Monthly payments are lower than on other mortgages.

Disadvantages. Unless you make provisions in the contract, the cost of all improvements comes out of your pocket. If they add to the value of the home and to the profit at time of sale, the lender shares in the extra profit, too. And because you're sharing the profit. you can get into some tricky tax situations with a SAM.

SHARED-EQUITY MORTGAGE. You get an investment partner in the form of a part-owner. The SEM can be an arms-length deal with an investor, a friend, a relative or anyone who wants to put up some cash in a piece of real estate in expectation of eventual profit, some depreciation, and tax deductions without the headaches of management of the physical property. You usually get to enjoy the use of the property as though you were sole owner. Your partner puts up all or part of the down payment and may share in the monthly payment.

Advantages. You need less money for the down payment and, in some cases, the monthly mortgage payments. A SEM can be a good arrangement with the right sort of partner and the right sort of legal agreement.

Disadvantages. There are some restrictions on

your ownership rights. You may be bound to buy out the investor at the end of a specified time, for example. You may also lose part of the interest deduction on your income taxes.

GROWING-EQUITY MORTGAGE. The GEM, a much later innovation than the unlimited ARM, has received a good deal of media attention. Basically a GEM is a plan for paying off a mortgage rapidly by systematically paying more on the principal. One type calls for mandatory fixed-percentage increases in the monthly payments, which are applied against the principal. That means that the entire increase in the payment goes into your pocket in the form of equity, instead of into the lender's in the form of interest. Some GEMs call for a fixed interest rate throughout the life of the loan; on others the rate changes. Different lenders offer different GEM plans, but all call for rapid payoff.

Actually, if the lender permits, other mortgages can be converted into GEMs. You simply make heftier payments on a voluntary rather than a mandatory basis. Once you have made your scheduled payment, anything extra—up to certain limits—is applied to the principal without penalty. Loans made by federal s&l's, for example, allow borrowers to prepay up to 20% of the original loan amount each year during the first five years. Making extra payments normally does not mean that you can then skip a regular payment.

Advantages. By all odds, this is one of the thriftiest of the new mortgages. With some plans your home is completely paid for in 12 to 15 years, half the time it takes to pay off most traditional fixed-rate loans. (See Table 4 at the end of this chapter for comparisons of the total interest paid on a typical GEM, a 30-year, fixed-rate mortgage and a graduated-payment mortgage.)

Disadvantages. A GEM may be harder to qualify for than a conventional fixed-rate loan. And paradoxically, the buyer who can best afford a GEM—the home buyer with high income—is less attracted to it because after the loan is five years old, he is making increasingly larger payments with decreasing amounts going for interest. That means a steadily shrinking tax deduction. Depending on how the individual GEM is structured, the interest part of the payment shrinks dramatically after the fifth or sixth year.

Payments can rise sharply in a GEM. With one lender's plan the payments in the 13th year are more than 50% higher than the first-year payments.

FIXED RATE WITH CALL OPTION. The lender may call in this mortgage at whatever time and for whatever reasons are spelled out in the contract. At the end of three years, for example, the lender may call the loan and set a new rate based on market rates at that time or refuse to renew at all. If you elect to keep the mortgage with the new rate, you keep that rate for whatever is left of the term. If you don't want the new rate, you'll have to pay off the loan by selling or refinancing.

Advantages. You lock in the initial rate for a specified period.

Disadvantages. You have no guarantee of what your eventual interest rate will be. If the market rate has risen by the time the loan is called in, your monthly outlays will rise.

BALLOON MORTGAGE. This loan usually has a series of monthly payments and a large final payment. Payments may cover interest only or both principal and interest. The unpaid balance, which could be more than the original amount of the loan, depending on the contract, is due at a specified time. Balloons are typically short-term mortgages.

The lender may or may not promise to refinance the loan when the balloon payment comes due. If he does, the new loan usually carries the current market rate.

Advantages. With most balloons you have predictable payments at a locked-in interest rate for five years or so.

Disadvantages. You are gambling that an affordable new loan will be available to you when you need it or that you'll be able to sell your home at that time.

ZERO INTEREST PLAN. The ZIP is a private arrangement between you and the seller (almost always a builder) to let you pay the total debt on your home in a relatively short period, say five or seven years. In return for such a rapid payoff, the builder agrees to charge no interest.

Advantages. You save a tremendous amount on interest cost. Furthermore, even though you're paying no interest, the IRS will allow you to impute a rate of 10% for tax purposes after the first six months of the payback period.

Disadvantages. A down payment of one-third to one-half is usually required. You must pay the remainder in equal installments, so the monthly load is heavy. Although the seller is charging no interest, you may be paying a premium on top of the price to compensate the seller for carrying you interest-free. Normally, the value of a home for tax purposes is the same as its price. With a ZIP, however, the cost basis—that is, the value from which gain or loss will be determined when you sell—is the stated price minus the imputed interest.

WHEN THE SELLER IS THE LENDER

For years sellers have been taking back notes from buyers who wanted to assume their first trust but didn't have enough cash to complete the deal. Such a note is called a second trust or second mortgage. Nearly always, that second trust had to be paid in full at the end of three, five or seven years. When mortgage money was plentiful, the buyer could refinance with ease and make that balloon payment.

The situation changed when interest rates soared and buyers couldn't find or afford a new mortgage to refinance their debt. The problem compounded: The harder it was to find a first mortgage, the more second trusts were used as brokers looked for ways to make new deals in a tight money market. But the same situation that gave rise to the ever-larger second trust made refinancing just as difficult. Everyone was betting on a better interest rate, which, for some, did not come in time. The second trust game is based on the expectation of a more affordable mortgage market down the road. In some cases buyers have also assumed they would be able to generate additional funds by refinancing a property that had appreciated substantially.

Most creative financing techniques involving sellers were created in response to hardships facing both buyers and sellers in a disastrously expensive mortgage market. It was clear that the second trust idea needed embellishment.

At their peak in late 1981 and mid 1982, seller financing arrangements accounted for about half of all sales on used homes. Since then several things have combined to reduce the demand for such financing: the introduction of the adjustable first mortgage, more and more legal barriers to the assumption of existing loans and, most important of all, a decline in interest rates that began in mid 1982.

DIRECT ASSUMPTION OF AN EXISTING LOAN. In an assumption the buyer takes over, or assumes, the payments on the seller's existing mortgage. This can be a distinct advantage when the interest rate on the seller's mortgage is considerably below current market rates. As a result, assumable mortgages constitute the cornerstone of much so-called creative financing.

Most conventional loans are not directly assumable, but any FHA or VA loan can be assumed by the buyer at the same rate. You have to check with the lender who made the mortgage; he may offer instead to give you a new loan with a moderate increase called a blended rate, described earlier in this chapter.

Don't try for a "silent" assumption of a loan that has a due-on-sale clause, which bars assumptions. Some buyers and sellers have sought to bypass due-on-sale clauses by not informing the lender of the sale. If the lender finds out you have made a quiet deal to avoid paying a higher interest rate, he can simply call in the loan. Then you will have to either qualify for his loan at the market rate or get one from another lender. If you can't qualify for a new loan, you might have to make a fast sacrifice sale to recoup what you have paid into the house.

Lenders are doubling and tripling their efforts to sniff out these unauthorized assumptions. They check the incoming mail carefully to see whether the check for the monthly payment is from their original borrower, for example. One sure tip-off to the lender is a change in the name on the homeowners insurance. If the buyer takes insurance in his own name, the lender will learn of it, since insurers routinely supply lenders with a copy of the notice of new insurance on property mortgaged. If the buyer foregoes having insurance in his own name, he runs the risk of losing all protection in the event of a fire or other casualty.

Lenders have another sleuthing device to catch unauthorized assumers of their loans. They routinely send promotional letters to their original borrowers at the property address. The letters might announce a new branch opening, mortgage life insurance or a new lending service. If the mail is intercepted at the post office and returned stamped "not at this address," the lender starts to investigate the whereabouts of his original borrower to see whether he has sold the property.

Advantages. In a market of high interest rates the rate on the assumable loan may be cheaper. More of your monthly payment may be applied to principal than might be the case with a new loan.

Disadvantages. The loan balance may be so low that by the time you add on a second trust payment large enough to cover the seller's equity, your total payment may be uncomfortably high.

THE CONTRACT SALE. This is a creative financing device that effects a kind of sale without disturbing the existing financing. Basically an installment sale, it is sometimes used in an attempt to thwart the due-on-sale clause in the seller's mortgage, even though that clause as used by most lenders also covers contract sales. In a contract sale title does not pass to the buyer until the terms of the contract are met, usually set for a time of the seller's choosing when the parties anticipate that favorable new financing will be available. The buyer usually makes a down payment and a monthly payment to the seller sufficient to cover the seller's mortgage and the new financing extended by the seller. It may be amortized as though it were a 20- or 30-year loan but have a balloon payment due in five or seven years. This sale is called a "contract for deed" in some areas.

Advantages. Like all creative financing, a contract sale can sometimes make possible a deal that wouldn't work with a commercial lender. It also uses the blended-rate approach, so the interest rate can be more favorable than it would be on a new loan.

Disadvantages. If strictly interpreted, this kind of contract offers little or no protection to the buyer. He can lose the property and his money if he is late with or fails to make a payment even though he may have already paid a large part of the purchase price. However, the courts and legislatures in a number of states have intervened on behalf of buyers in an effort to obtain fairer treatment for them.

Unless the contract is properly handled, the buyer cannot be sure his payments will be applied to the underlying loan or that real estate taxes will be paid. He may have no protection against liens. A contract sale leaves the buyer in an insecure position because he does not take title until the contract is paid off and cannot be sure what the condition of the title will be at that time.

No contract sale should be entered into without the advice of a real estate attorney and the buyer should require a title insurance policy.

All schemes designed to thwart the due-on-sale clause, including the option to buy discussed below, that are based on the owner's retaining the title are risky for the buyer. Some due-on-sale clauses specifically bar contract sales. In such a case the lender may call in the loan if he discovers what has been done.

THE WRAPAROUND. This is another application of the blended rate technique and works only where the loan is assumable. With this plan the existing loan is not replaced by a new one, as in the case of the blend, but instead the old loan is kept and new money is added to it, or wrapped around it. A wraparound might be made by a commercial lender or the seller. The principle of a wraparound is that it takes advantage of a low interest rate on an existing mortgage, thereby reducing the amount of new money at high rates needed to complete the transaction.

Suppose you're interested in a property selling for $100,000. The seller is holding a 9% mortgage on the place with a balance of $50,000. You can put $20,000 down. The seller makes you this offer: He will keep his mortgage in place and lend you the $80,000 you need at a rate of 12%. The market rate at the time is 14%, so naturally you jump at the chance. But what's in it for the seller?

Just this: You will be making payments to him as if you had borrowed $80,000. Your payments to him are $823 per month on a 30-year loan. Out of that he makes his old mortgage payment, which, assuming his original mortgage was $60,000, amounts to $483 a month on a 30-year loan. After paying his mortgage, he pockets $340 a month, which represents his return on the $30,000 difference between what he owes and what he lends you. Multiplying $340 by 12 gives him an annual return of $4,080. On an outlay of $30,000, that works out to an annual return of almost 14%.

There are other ways of figuring the return on wraparound loans, and other ways of packaging them, but you can see from the example why they would be attractive to both buyers and sellers.

Advantages. Both the interest rate and the monthly

payment may be less than if new financing were sought for the total price of the house, and more of your payments may go toward principal. You can also expect to pay less for a wraparound than if you assumed the old loan and secured a conventional second trust.

Disadvantages. The buyer may have no assurance that the underlying loan will be paid unless payments are handled by a commercial lender or an escrow agent. Good candidates for such a deal are hard to find. Even though the seller retains his old mortgage, in effect you are assuming it. Therefore, the existing loan must be assumable. FHA and VA loans are prime candidates.

In some cities very aggressive mortgage lenders compile lists of homes for sale that have assumable mortgages or mortgages that are candidates for a blended rate. They make up these lists by culling the multiple listing service and distribute the information to agents and prospective buyers. Ask your agent.

LEASE WITH AN OPTION TO BUY. With this arrangement you are renting with the right to buy at some future date. Most lease-options involve short-term leases of one to two years. To get the option, you would generally have to put up $1,000 to $2,000, but the money would be applied toward the purchase if you exercise the option. Part or all of the rental payments may also be credited toward the purchase price. If the option is not exercised, you'd probably have to forfeit everything you'd paid. It's important to have the contract prepared by a real estate attorney experienced in this kind of arrangement.

Advantages. You are not committed to the purchase unless you decide to exercise the option. The arrangement might allow you to wait out a period of high interest rates and buy the property with a more advantageous loan at a locked-in price. Your contract may allow you to extend or sell and assign the option.

Disadvantages. These deals are most common in depressed markets or for property that is hard to sell. You may have to pay an above-the-market rent. You could lose the money you paid for the option if you don't buy and can't sell it to someone else while the option is still in effect. Often you have no assurance of what the price will be.

LEASE-PURCHASE. A lease-purchase obligates the buyer to purchase the property at an agreed-upon price and at an agreed-upon date. The lease and the sales contract are usually written at the same time, and the settlement date will correspond to the expiration of the lease. Regular rental payments are made to the seller during the life of the lease.

Advantages. The buyer locks in the future price of the home. He also has time to shop for financing and to accumulate the down payment.

Disadvantages. You may pay a higher rent and you will not have interest deductions while you are leasing. If you back down, you could be sued for breach of contract. If at settlement time the seller could not provide the kind of title required in the sales contract, you would not have to conclude the sale but you would have wasted both time and money.

Table 1

ADJUSTABLE-RATE MORTGAGES

How payments could go up or down

Say you have a $90,000 loan at an initial rate of 13½%. Here's what the monthly payments would be in a fully amortized loan if interest rates *rose* ½ of 1% every five years and payments are adjusted every five years. (Figures were supplied by Delson Financial Mortgage Bankers.)

years	rate and amortization period	monthly payment	principal balance at end of period
1–5	13½% for 30 yrs.	$1,031.40	$88,394.40
6–10	14% for 25 yrs.	1,064.27	85,553.40
11–15	14½% for 20 yrs.	1,095.08	80,193.48
16–20	15% for 15 yrs.	1,122.71	69,532.56
21–25	15½% for 10 yrs.	1,143.81	47,465.01
26–30	16% for 5 yrs.	1,154.35	–0–

And this is what the monthly payments would be if interest rates *dropped* ½ of 1% every five years.

years	rate and amortization period	monthly payment	principal balance at end of term
1–5	13½% for 30 yrs.	$1,031.40	$88,394.40
6–10	13% for 25 yrs.	997.09	85,081.38
11–15	12½% for 20 yrs.	967.38	78,373.56
16–20	12% for 15 yrs.	941.27	65,511.68
21–25	11½% for 10 yrs.	921.09	41,878.34
26–30	11% for 5 yrs.	910.85	–0–

Table 2
GRADUATED-PAYMENT MORTGAGES
How they compare with fixed-rate loans

This graduated-payment mortgage for $90,000 at 13½% has a predetermined payment schedule and negative amortization. The early payments start low, at 10⅛%, and then gradually catch up to the level necessary to amortize the loan. In this loan the last 25 years would be at approximately 15⅛%. The monthly payment for a comparable loan on a straight 30-year, fixed-rate mortgage (FRM) would be $1,031.40, for a total of $12,376.80 annually.

year	payment	difference from FRM	total paid annually
1	$ 800.26	$231.14 less	$ 9,603.12
2	860.28	171.12 less	10,323.36
3	924.80	106.60 less	11,097.60
4	994.15	37.25 less	11,929.80
5	1,068.72	37.32 more	12,834.64
6–30	1,148.87	117.47 more for 25 years	

After the fifth year the borrower owes $98,560.76, or $8,560.76 more than he did originally. The payment is adjusted every year until the sixth year, when the final adjustment is made. The payment for years 6 through 30 is roughly 11⅛% greater than it would be with a 30-year, fixed-rate loan ($1,148.78 vs. $1,031.40.)

The convenience of having smaller payments for the first four years doesn't come cheap.

Total payments on GPM	$400,439.52
Total payments on FRM	371,304.00
Extra cost of GPM	$ 29,135.52

Table 3

TRACKING FIVE YEARS' WORTH OF PAYMENTS

Here are hypothetical examples of three kinds of variable mortgages for a $60,000, 30-year loan. They demonstrate what could happen to the monthly payment in a period as volatile as 1979 to 1982.

Example No. 1: *Rate and payment adjustment once each year with no cap*

year	rate	payment	balance
1	10.94%	$568.68	$60,000.00
2	12.00	616.59	59,726.40
3	15.38	773.06	59,481.30
4	14.75	743.63	59,343.30
5	16.00	801.67	59,160.90
6	17.00	848.22	58,994.70
7	18.00	894.78	58,832.90

Example No. 2: *Rate and payment adjustment every three years in an amortizing loan with no cap*

years	rate	payment	balance
1–3	10.94%	$568.68	$60,000.00
3–6	14.75	740.35	59,081.30
6–9	18.00	888.90	58,445.90

Example No. 3: *Rate adjustment every six months, payment adjustment every five years*
There is a 25% cap on payment adjustments. If a payment is insufficient to pay the interest due, the loan balance is increased in the form of negative amortization.

month	rate	payment	balance
1	10.94%	$568.68	$60,000.00
6	15.11	568.68	59,866.90
12	10.56	568.68	61,013.40
18	12.77	568.68	60,818.60
24	14.91	568.68	61,302.50
30	12.75	568.68	62,497.20
36	9.38	568.68	63,084.70
42	9.88	568.68	62,622.40
48	10.38	568.68	62,297.20
54	10.88	568.68	62,114.50
60	11.38	625.59	62,080.70
66	11.88	625.59	61,854.20
72	12.38	625.59	61,772.80

Table 4

HOW A GEM SLASHES INTEREST COSTS

The total interest cost of a growing-equity mortgage (GEM) is less than half that of two other loans on a $67,500 mortgage at 13%.

year	payment number	Growing Equity		30-Year, Fixed Rate		Graduated Payment	
		payment	principal balance	payment	principal balance	payment	principal balance
1	12	$ 747	$67,303	$747	$67,303	$578	$69,454
2	24	777	66,699	747	67,080	621	71,125
3	36	808	65,616	747	66,825	668	72,432
5	60	874	61,671	747	66,206	772	73,564
10	120	1,063	35,991	747	63,735	830	70,818
13	156	1,195	2,908	747	61,357	830	68,085
14	159	477	0	747	61,020	830	67,805
TOTAL INTEREST		$84,442		$201,286		$221,694	

Table 5

WHAT WILL THE PAYMENTS BE ON A FIXED-RATE LOAN?

This table allows you to calculate your monthly mortgage payment for each $1,000 of mortgage amount at common interest rates over four mortgage periods. Principal and interest are included; insurance and property taxes would be additional expenses. To calculate your monthly payment for a new mortgage, multiply the amount in the appropriate column by the number of thousands of dollars involved. Example: For a 30-year loan of $60,000 at 12% interest, multiply 60 by $10.29. The monthly payment equals $617.40.

interest rate	15 years	20 years	25 years	30 years
9 %	$10.15	$ 9.00	$ 8.40	$ 8.05
9¼	10.30	9.16	8.57	8.23
9½	10.45	9.33	8.74	8.41
9¾	10.60	9.49	8.92	8.60
10	10.75	9.66	9.09	8.78
10¼	10.90	9.82	9.27	8.97
10½	11.06	9.99	9.45	9.15
10¾	11.21	10.16	9.63	9.34
11	11.37	10.33	9.81	9.53
11¼	11.53	10.50	9.99	9.72
11½	11.69	10.67	10.17	9.91
11¾	11.85	10.84	10.35	10.10
12	12.01	11.02	10.54	10.29
12¼	12.17	11.19	10.72	10.48
12½	12.33	11.37	10.91	10.68
12¾	12.49	11.54	11.10	10.87
13	12.66	11.72	11.28	11.07
13¼	12.82	11.90	11.47	11.26
13½	12.99	12.08	11.66	11.46
13¾	13.15	12.26	11.85	11.66
14	13.32	12.44	12.04	11.85
14¼	13.49	12.62	12.23	12.05

interest rate	15 years	20 years	25 years	30 years
14½%	$13.66	$12.80	$12.43	$12.25
14¾	13.83	12.99	12.62	12.45
15	14.00	13.17	12.81	12.65
15¼	14.17	13.36	13.01	12.85
15½	14.34	13.54	13.20	13.05
15¾	14.52	13.73	13.40	13.25
16	14.69	13.92	13.59	13.45
16¼	14.87	14.11	13.79	13.65
16½	15.04	14.29	13.99	13.86
16¾	15.22	14.48	14.18	14.06
17	15.40	14.67	14.38	14.26
17¼	15.57	14.86	14.58	14.46
17½	15.75	15.05	14.78	14.67
17¾	15.93	15.25	14.98	14.87
18	16.11	15.44	15.18	15.08
18¼	16.29	15.63	15.38	15.28
18½	16.47	15.82	15.58	15.48
18¾	16.65	16.02	15.78	15.69
19	16.83	16.21	15.98	15.89
19¼	17.02	16.41	16.18	16.10
19½	17.20	16.60	16.39	16.30
19¾	17.38	16.80	16.59	16.51
20	17.57	16.99	16.79	16.72

CHECKLIST FOR COMPARING MORTGAGE LOANS

Check types and lenders against each other

After you have been prequalified for the amount of money you may borrow, use these forms to compare *types* of loans. After you have identified the one or two kinds of loans that interest you, compare the terms and costs of several lenders.

What kind of loan is it?	fixed rate ☐
	adjustable ☐

For fixed-rate

What is the percentage rate?	_____ %
How many years?	_____ years
Cost in points	$_____
Is it callable by the lender before the end of its term?	
	☐ yes ☐ no
If so, when?	in _____ years
Is there a prepayment penalty?	☐ yes ☐ no
How much?	$_____
Is it assumable at the same rate?	☐ yes ☐ no
	☐ at a blended rate?

For adjustable loans

Adjustables *Without* Ceilings

Beginning interest rate   _____%

Beginning payment $_____

Cost in points $_____

Loan is tied to which index?

6-month Treasury bills ☐

1-year Treasury securities ☐

3-year Treasury securities ☐

5-year Treasury securities ☐

Federal Home Loan Bank Board (FHLBB) series

for closed loans on existing homes ☐

other index ☐

adjustments are made every _____ months

_____ years

first payment adjustment date _____

Adjustables *With* Ceilings

Beginning interest rate   _____%

Beginning payment $_____

Cost in points $_____

Is there a cap on the interest rate?   ☐ yes   ☐ no

What is the cap?   _____%

Is there a cap on the payment?   ☐ yes   ☐ no

What is the cap? $_____

Loan is tied to which index?

6-month Treasury bills ☐

1-year Treasury securities ☐

3-year Treasury securities ☐

5-year Treasury securities ☐

Federal Home Loan Bank Board (FHLBB) series

for closed loans on existing homes ☐

other index ☐

1st adjustment occurs _____ months/years

2nd adjustment occurs _____ months/years

3rd adjustment occurs _____ months/years

4th adjustment occurs _____ months/years

5th adjustment occurs _____ months/years

Loan calls for _____ adjustments

Loan provides for negative amortization ☐ yes ☐ no

Is there a limit on the negative amortization?

☐ yes ☐ no

Interest rate stabilizes in _____th year

Monthly payment stabilizes in _____th year

5

Planning Your House Hunt

Strategy and tactics

Buying a piece of real estate is a science. Buying a home is an art. The science is getting the legal and financial part right. The art is finding a property that you can be happy living in.

You can hire all the help you need with the technical side, but a little serious homework will eliminate much of the mystery. It will also help you to use the advice you buy, whether it is from an accountant, lawyer or appraiser.

The nontechnical side is another matter. Only you know what you like. If you don't decide what you like before you go into the market, someone out there in that market is going to try to make up your mind for you, and you might not be happy with the results.

Unhappy results can be anything from accepting something you don't really like much to quitting in disgust or despair.

The key to success is to act on the market; don't let it act on you.

If you do your preparation before you enter the market, you can win, even when prices and mortgage rates are high.

ANXIETY ATTACKS

Faced with the challenge of making what often is the largest investment they have ever made, buyers sometimes react in a variety of anxious ways.

Some get preoccupied with becoming an expert on housing components. This is the manufactured-item approach, and it is much like researching the purchase of a car or TV: What is the best heating/cooling system? Which type of roof has the longest life? What size copper should the plumbing be? And on and on.

The danger of this approach is that you are likely to get fixated on components and go out and buy the best components instead of the best house. You could end up with a Mercedes-quality heating plant in a Pinto house.

Component shoppers get so carried away with their project that they refuse to look at any property that doesn't have their favorite component. This is getting things backward. You should never buy a home *because* of its heating plant, although you might be smart to buy a particular house *despite* its heating plant.

Other buyers get preoccupied with structural defects. They had an uncle who once bought a house with a cracked foundation, or they have been poring over books that are more about construction than real estate. They are determined to ferret out the sinking foundation, the hidden roof leak or the uneven floor. The trouble with this approach is that while they are scaring themselves to death over normal aging cracks, they are missing the things they should be looking for: Is this the right size, the right feel and the right area for me? There's time enough for the construction diagnosis later.

Another kind of buyer gets hung up on the size of the deposit or the fear of getting taken in by the fine print in the sales contract before he even finds the home. Still another is absorbed with the condition of the dishwasher, the wall oven and the garbage disposer and gravitates toward homes with a warranty, thereby often passing up a superior property just because it didn't come with an appliance warranty.

This is not to say that any of those concerns are unimportant, but they shouldn't dominate the search or determine what you will look at and what you won't. Concentrate on the rightness or the wrongness of the total property. Have the components diagnosed after you have made a tentative selection.

Probably the most common mistake buyers make is to become preoccupied with price. The time to have professional help on whether a property is fairly priced is after you have made a selection. It is a serious mistake to become so obsessed with dollar signs that you get detoured from your main purpose, which is to search out properties that seem to offer what you need. This doesn't mean you should pay no attention to price range as you shop; it only means you shouldn't rule something out because the asking price seems to be 10% or 15% too high. It may or may not be. If it is, negotiating might be able to take care of that later.

The price-preoccupied buyer is so determined not to pay one penny over market value that he screens every property according to whether the price is right instead of whether it is the right property. This is all the more ironic when you consider that three professional appraisers often set three different market values on the same property. The "right" price is really a right range, not a single objective, discoverable fact. It is the meeting place between a willing buyer and a willing seller, subject to the continuing changes the market brings.

Anxieties are understandable in a buyer faced with a very large purchase and a very long commitment and the uneasy feeling that nobody is on his side.

He knows the broker's commission comes from the seller's funds (though paid indirectly by the buyer in the price), so the broker is beholden to the seller. By law the broker and the agent have a fiduciary responsibility to the seller. Their legal obligation to the buyer is much more limited. They must tell the truth and be honest in the handling of his funds. But they have no obligation to counsel, guide or instruct the buyer, or to protect him from his own folly.

This concern sends some home seekers to the law books, where they get heavily involved with the principles of real property and draft themselves a lengthy contract full of legalese. But an iron-clad contract is no guarantee they won't wind up with a bum house.

A few would-be buyers decide that the way to beat

the system is to learn the system, so they enroll in real estate classes, where they are drilled, along with the future pros, on how to pass the examination for a real estate license, an exercise that is largely useless in a home search.

Then there are the buyers who are convinced that field research, not theory, is the answer. Their approach is to look at every property on the market. They overindulge in information and end up with a painful case of indecision.

All of this is time-consuming, enervating and self-defeating.

KNOW YOUR NEEDS

Your best preparation for home buying is to be clear about your needs, your pocketbook, your preferences and your prejudices.

The central questions are what kind of home do you want and where do you want it?

If you are clear on those things, you will be immune to pressure tactics and hype. You will be better able to evaluate the style of the agents you meet and weed out the pushers, the cajolers and the indifferent.

You will soon discover that the better you have defined your housing goals in terms of not just what you can afford but also what you want, the better your chances of finding an efficient agent. If you are too vague, the really good agents may decide not to waste time on you, and you'll end up with the kind who are more hindrance than help. They may have endless patience, but they have no direction.

Knowing your financial limits is a necessary beginning, but it is only a beginning. You could, and probably will, be offered 15 or 20 entirely different sorts of homes, all within your price range. You need to make decisions in advance about whether you want to be on the east or west side, whether you want to be in a development or would go to any lengths to avoid that, whether you want to or can handle a "fix-up." Otherwise, you're in for confusion when you find the living room you want in a house on the west side and the school district you want on the east side.

It can't be overstated: *Keep an eye on the location and general quality of the property.* Don't go chasing the right price or the right furnace. Making those things right is what negotiation is all about.

If you rush out prematurely with this or that requirement, you may just satisfy it, whether the house or neighborhood is right or not. There is a kind of agent who, learning that a buyer has a fixation about a heat pump, or a den with a south exposure, or a one-bedroom, three-bath house, will follow that specification requirement even if it takes him to a house in the shadow of an underpass or next to a supermarket warehouse.

There are two phases to a home-seeking expedition. In the first, you are getting the feel for different areas and a feel for what is being offered at what price. From that you draw up a list of specifications. The second phase is the search to fill those specifications.

YOUR MUST LIST VS. YOUR WANT LIST

The final choice of a home almost always requires compromising. What makes it tough is that one home will have part of what you want, a second home will have another part, and maybe a third will have another part. It helps if you sift out what is necessary for you and rank what is merely desirable before you get to that choosing point.

	MUSTS	WANTS (rank) high	medium	low
commuting time:				
less than one hour	____	____	____	____
less than half-hour	____	____	____	____
particular neighborhood	____	____	____	____
particular architectural style	____	____	____	____
1 story, 2 stories, split level	____	____	____	____
urban setting	____	____	____	____
country feeling	____	____	____	____
number of bedrooms	____	____	____	____
eat-in kitchen	____	____	____	____
separate dining room	____	____	____	____
basement	____	____	____	____
expandability	____	____	____	____
particular school district	____	____	____	____
public transportation	____	____	____	____

economy: fix-up house	___	___	___	___
energy efficiency	___	___	___	___
fireplace	___	___	___	___
other: _____	___	___	___	___
_____	___	___	___	___
_____	___	___	___	___
_____	___	___	___	___
_____	___	___	___	___

DEFINING YOUR IDEAL

On any given day in any given city, if people actively looking in the house market were asked, What kind of house are you looking for?, the overwhelming majority of the responses would name the number of bedrooms they want. Some would add a price limit, and a few might also give a general location.

Starting with such a vague list of requirements without any real specifics to pinpoint the search is what makes house hunting such a miserable chore.

In a large city, there might easily be 100 or more three-bedroom houses for sale at any given time. The probabilities are that if a buyer were so prodigal with his time as to look at all 100, he would find 90 of them inappropriate for him. That is the kind of odds you can expect if you let enticing ads swerve you off course.

Experienced agents—those who have shown hundreds and even thousands of houses—know that most buyers are in search of something they cannot describe. They may be trying, often unknowingly, to replicate a childhood home, if it was a happy one. If it wasn't happy, whatever stands out about that home goes on the buyer's negative list.

This doesn't mean that they are looking for the same red-brick corner house with privet hedge, but rather they seek a feeling, an ambience. It could be a feeling of spaciousness, warmth, airiness, the amount of daylight, the quality of the light, coziness, the abundance of nooks and crannies, a parklike backyard.

Though the following trick won't work for everybody, it does provide a clue on how to start to build a "want" list. Recall the houses you have liked and write down a description of each. If you have already determined your price range, that combined with your want list will give you a sieve through which you can sift the dozens and dozens of ads you will read in conducting your search. Without a well-defined want list you will be doomed to the bumbling typical of the unprepared buyer.

With nothing more than enticing ads telling how easy it is to move right in, the unprogrammed buyer can in a single weekend of driving around wander into a $250,000 detached home in a "nice" neighborhood; a condominium with the enticing price of $69,500 with 10% down but remodeled in a slapdash manner; a dull little house with a tired exterior and a dreary interior but priced just right (the ad said it could be the perfect "starter home" with a minor face-lift); and finally, a fairly interesting house on a fairly good street, but somewhat overpriced at $125,000.

Soon your phone is ringing more and more. The condominium salesman is calling once a day because he wants to show you another unit in the same complex, a corner unit this time, and when you reject that, one on the south side, then one on the tenth floor, and so on.

The saleswoman with the $250,000 house refuses to believe you can't afford it and wants you to "come back and look one more time."

The agent with the tired little house suggests that maybe the seller would agree to cut the price enough to pay for redecorating inside and out.

The agent who showed the house with the almost-right price calls back and says it has been sold, so how about looking at a new one he has on "about as good a street at a slightly higher price."

If you go out a second and third time with this crew, meanwhile adding more input of your own as you drop in on open houses, you will be reacting to features in perhaps two dozen offerings.

Sound like a good start? It's a terrible start. None of the two dozen are comparable. The more entries you add in this haphazard manner, the more confused you'll become.

Buyers who follow that approach become spoiled instead of educated. They've seen the spacious living room, the big entrance hall, and the extra storage space in the expensive house, and unconsciously they are trying to duplicate it in a much lower price range with no major sacrifice in location. If they look for a year, they won't be able to do that, but they keep on trying. What's worse, they have seen the price and term delights of a cheap property: less than $7,000 down for the condominium. They wouldn't be happy a week, or even a day, in that badly renovated condominium, but the pleasant sound of $7,000 keeps ringing in their ears. There was nothing particularly compelling about the almost-right house on the almost-right street, so the lesson implicit in the fact that someone else quickly snatched it up probably escapes them. Using the stumbling technique, it may take them several months more of unprogrammed shopping before their judgment is developed enough to recognize the value of the next almost-right property.

The "almost" aspect is important. Buyers often have the hopelessly naive idea that they are going to find everything they want in a single package, and so they keep dragging through the market in hopes of finding it. They haven't learned yet that buying a home is a process of making compromises. The smart buyer knows what to compromise on and where to hold firm. The foolish buyer wanders around not quite sure of what he is looking for. The old "I'll just keep looking, I'll know it when I see it" routine may work in department stores and specialty shops, but it is a poor way to shop for a home.

Why is the stumbling routine so inappropriate for house hunting? Because the market is too vast and there are too many variables, many of which are not discernible by the superficial shopper. The picture never clears for him; instead, it clouds up because the houses he visits are in no way comparable.

Sooner or later, such a buyer will end up in his price range. The market will force him there. The pity is that by the time he gets there, he may have passed his level of tolerance for frustration. It is not at all unusual for a buyer who has shopped in this helter-skelter fashion to buy just anything that fits his purse. Sadly, he could have done better with less but better-directed effort.

WHY THE "PERFECT" HOME TURNS SOUR

Say you have a well-defined want list, you screen ads carefully, you instruct every agent you work with, and you refuse to look at any property that doesn't have the requisite fireplace, family room, entrance hall or whatever your firm requirements are. After weeks, perhaps months, of looking, the seemingly perfect home shows up. It has every one of the items on your want list.

First there is euphoria over finding all the desired features in one package. Then, to the bewilderment of the agent or the seller of this perfect home, you go silent. You may announce, "I need more time to think it over." That thinking-it-over time might take hours, days, maybe even a week. At last your final answer is no.

Why does the perfect home fail to win the only test that counts: whether, when it comes right down to crunch time, you are unwilling to plunk down a deposit? The reason may be that you failed to identify your "don't wants."

Finding a home with all the desired features is only half the battle. The property must also be free from objectionable features.

This is especially difficult for some couples, who may not hold the same objections. A woman may feel strongly about the traffic in front of the house, for example, while the man is relatively indifferent to it and unwilling to pass up an otherwise perfect home because of it.

Objections, which constitute a don't-want list, are of two major types: personal prejudice and economic fear. And there's plenty of overlap between the two.

Probably as many homes are purchased for their freedom from objectionable features as are bought for positive reasons. This is particularly true in the lower price ranges. Sometimes the purchase is concluded despite the reservations of one or both of the buyers, to their later regret. This often accounts for quick turnarounds—instances when new owners put their home back on the market before they have barely settled in.

IDENTIFY YOUR VETO ZONES

If you were considering homes that matched these descriptions, how would you react? Even more important, how closely do your answers coincide with those of your spouse or home-buying partner? If one of you can accept something that would be a major drawback to the other, you'd better know it before you do much shopping.

THIS HOUSE (OR CONDOMINIUM APART-
MENT) LOOKS PRETTY MUCH IDENTICAL TO
THE OTHERS ON THE STREET (OR IN THE
AREA).

( ) I can't stand that.
( ) Looks like a real community.
( ) So what?

IT SEEMS DARK. THERE IS VERY LITTLE
DAYLIGHT.

( ) That's depressing.
( ) It seems peaceful.
( ) It doesn't matter. I'm never home days, any-
way.

THIS HOME IS IN A PRETTY CLUBBY NEIGH-
BORHOOD (OR APARTMENT COMPLEX). IT
SEEMS LIKE THERE IS A LOT OF SOCIALIZ-
ING AMONG THE NATIVES.

( ) Good, I like a built-in social life.
( ) Let me out. I want more privacy than that.
( ) I can take it or leave it.

IT'S A GREAT PLACE, BUT IT'S 35 MILES
FROM WORK.

( ) That's too much commuting for me.
( ) If you want something sharp at a good price,
you have to drive for it.
( ) I like living in a totally different atmosphere
from where I work.
( ) I would prefer to be closer in, but I might go
for it anyway.

IT'S JUST WHAT I WANT, BUT EVEN AFTER ALL THAT HAGGLING, IT'S STILL OVER MY BUDGET.

- ( ) It's worth it. I'll stretch and give up something else.
- ( ) Too bad, but I have to draw the line somewhere. Let's start looking again.
- ( ) If I can't have this, I give up. I haven't the heart to look anymore.

I DON'T REALLY LIKE IT ALL THAT MUCH, BUT IT'S DECENT, AND WE CAN AFFORD IT.

- ( ) It's okay for a starter home.
- ( ) It's much tackier than anything I've ever lived in, but I could get used to it.
- ( ) Count me out. I'd rather stick it out in a rented apartment until we can afford something better.

THE AGENT SAYS THIS PROPERTY IS A REAL DIAMOND IN THE ROUGH. EVEN WITH THE COST OF REMODELING, WE'D STILL BE WAY AHEAD OF THE GAME, AND IT WOULD BE WHAT WE WANT.

- ( ) Looks good to me. With a paint job, a new kitchen and new baths, it will be terrific.
- ( ) It's too much of an unknown. Heaven knows what kind of horrible surprises await anyone who starts tearing into that old place. And suppose it costs twice as much as the estimates?
- ( ) I can do a lot of the work myself. We'll live in it "as is" and fix it up as we go.

( ) No thanks. I couldn't stand living in the midst of all that remodeling upheaval and dirt—and I wouldn't sleep in it one night "as is."

INTERESTING HOUSE AND THE PRICE IS RIGHT, BUT THE NEIGHBORHOOD LOOKS A LITTLE SHAKY.

( ) Not for me. I think location is as important as the house.

( ) It's not that shaky. Anyway, it's a lot more house than we could afford in a prime neighborhood.

( ) I'm not so sure. The neighborhood may be picking up, but living there in the meantime would seem like an eternity.

GREAT SPACE, GOOD FLOOR PLAN, BUT IT'S SO CHEAPLY BUILT. *EVERYTHING* IS ECONOMY GRADE.

( ) Count me out. I'd fume every time I tried to hang a picture and the wall shook.

( ) It's not such a bad compromise. It's not costing a fortune, either.

( ) If we loaded it up with expensive furniture and draperies, it would look okay.

BEST HOUSE FOR THE MONEY WE'VE SEEN, NO DOUBT ABOUT IT. BUT THE TRAFFIC ON THIS STREET IS HEAVY.

( ) It's too dangerous for kids.

( ) It's too noisy.

( ) Doesn't bother me. It's quiet enough at night.

FASCINATING HOUSE, GOOD PRICE, BUT IT'S SO CLOSE TO THAT SHOPPING CENTER (or parking lot, school, church, gas station, public utility station, office building or restaurant).

( ) Think what it would cost if it weren't.

( ) It spoils the residential character for me.

( ) That worries me. It might be hard to sell if we had to.

( ) Not for me. Once that commercial world starts moving in, there's no telling how far it will go.

IT'S A CUSTOM HOUSE ALL RIGHT. BEAUTIFULLY MADE. BUT IT'S THE ONLY ONE LIKE IT ON THE STREET. EVERYTHING ELSE IS PRETTY CHEAP.

( ) Fine with me to be king of the mountain. What do I care about the other houses?

( ) I would be leery of any property that's too good for its neighborhood.

I LIKE THIS HOUSE, BUT THERE ISN'T A KID IN SIGHT IN THE NEIGHBORHOOD.

( ) We had better pass. Who would ours play with?

( ) *Marvelous!* After working all day, the last thing I want to come home to is yelling kids and barking dogs.

PINPOINT YOUR PREJUDICES

To avoid getting yourself into a situation where you have to veto a house that has everything you say you want, you need to search systematically through your prejudices about places to live.

Go back through your past again, and this time think of all the homes you have *not* liked, whether you lived in them or merely visited them. Include ones occupied by friends, acquaintances, family—all the houses and apartments that for one physical reason or another made a negative impression on you. If they gave you a "I wouldn't want to have to live here" feeling, now is the time to identify that feeling. *Make a written list of the things you didn't like.*

Identify your personal objections, whatever they are: inside kitchens, small bathrooms, northern exposures, frame construction, casement windows, dormers, asbestos tile flooring, fake brick siding, living room full of doors, railroad-car floor plan, shoddy construction, scary neighborhood, too little daylight, house incongruous with its surroundings, too far out, too much of a child-rearing neighborhood, too much of an all-adult atmosphere, proximity to a commercial or industrial zone, deadend street, heavy traffic, street with no trees, street with overgrown trees, whatever.

Also consider things that other buyers might object to. Heavy traffic on the street may not bother you, but it's legitimate to be concerned that it might make resale tougher.

Other buyers might also balk at buying your house if it's overimproved or overbuilt. A home may have great entertaining space, a swimming pool and artistic landscaping—all features that are normally attractive to upscale buyers. But if the house is the only upgraded home in an area of ordinary homes, it will not be attractive to the typical high-income buyer. That makes it an interesting white elephant, and it could be a terrific bargain if you can negotiate the price down to reflect the home's wrong location. Such bargains can be deceptive though: sweet on the buying end and sour on the selling end. That may not matter to you if you are practically certain that you will not need to sell it before you can afford to take either no profit or a loss.

After you have your list of things you don't want in a home, assign them weights. Decide which objections are negotiable and which aren't. You might, for example, give in for a house with a western garden when you really wanted a southern one, but you would not give in on a heavily trafficked street.

If you are buying a home with a spouse or a partner, compare your don't-want lists. Frequently, the person with the strongest objections is the silent partner of the team. The more vocal one may take the lead in putting together the "want" list, but when it comes down to crunch time, it is the usually silent one who produces a veto, often for an objection not voiced before or not even thought about before.

Besides being destructive of the home-hunting process, these out-of-the-blue vetoes can put terrific strains on a relationship. Agents, mortgage loan interviewers and escrow agents never cease to be amazed at how a couple may know all about each other's tastes in food, vacations, cars, clothes and entertainment and not know about strongly held prejudices about a permanent place to live. Since rental apartment living is so often a matter of expediency or convenience anyway, it doesn't offer an adequate test. Taking the time to avoid this sort of surprise is more than worth it.

Objections are much more elusive than demands because they don't get thought about or talked about as much. But if you know yours, as well as their relative importance, you will be way ahead in the home-hunting game.

DECODING THE CLASSIFIED ADS

Classified ads are designed more to entice than to inform.

One good by-product of inflation, so far as the real estate consumer is concerned, is the steadily rising cost of newspaper advertising. Nothing has done so much to reduce the windy lyricism of home-selling advertisements.

Now a new challenge appears. With advertising getting so expensive, ads are getting more and more terse, some of them so abbreviated as to be nearly unintelligible. After a while you get the hang of "2b, 1½ba, lctm, owc, q.pos.," but it takes a while: two bedrooms, 1½ baths, low cash to mortgage, owner will carry back financing, quick possession.

Good or bad, straightforward or flowery, classified ads are an important channel of communication between home buyers and sellers, whether the advertisers are do-it-yourselfers or brokers.

Word-of-mouth advertising and "For Sale" signs planted in front yards sell plenty of houses, but the classified ad section is an important bulletin board offering a view of the day-to-day offerings in the residential real estate market.

Typically, resale homes are offered in the classified ads and new homes in large display ads. The classifieds are thrown at you in random fashion. In large cities they may be grouped by geographic areas and perhaps by price range. That helps somewhat, but within those categories there is great volume and diversity even in a middle-sized town. Large firms often run umbrella ads with all their offerings in one large ad, further complicating your task.

To use the classified ads successfully, you have to be prepared for the game. The aim is to get you into the advertised property by telling you only the things that might attract you there while withholding, or at least not offering, the information that might discourage you.

That is why the conversation with an agent answering your telephone inquiry can be so maddening. Rather than tell you what you want to know about a house's style or condition or roominess, a large percentage of agents will play coy: "Oh, come and see it; you'll just love it."

Not uncommon is the paranoid agent who suspects every caller is a rival broker: "Are you an agent?"

Then there is the terse one who isn't about to give away any information without some commitment from you: "If you want to come and see the property, I'll be glad to tell you all about it."

The opposite type, just as frustrating, will spend a lot of time describing everything down to the print on the shelf lining of the kitchen cabinets, all before mentioning the financing.

And then there's the agent who will manage, in four or five exchanges, to extract from you how much you have to pay down, your price range, how long you have looked, and with whom you have looked.

How useful are the classified ads in your search? It can be invaluable in helping you survey the entire city if you are starting out with no fixed ideas of where you want to buy. A few weeks of discriminating ad reading can give you a good indication of price ranges and flavors of neighborhoods. It can also acquaint you with the brokerage firms that specialize in various areas and, sometimes, the individual agent who specializes in a particular kind of house.

The classified ad section is even more valuable once you zero in on one or two areas. With the classified ads you can keep current on new offerings and price reductions as well as probable sales when certain ads disappear. If you work at it diligently, you can become your own market expert in a relatively short time. If you know how long a property has been advertised, what its starting price was and how many real estate firms have offered it, you have a considerable leg up in the negotiating process when you're ready to make an offer.

How to read an ad. First you analyze the ad for what it does say and then you study it for what it doesn't say.

Ads offer such different sorts of information that it requires real concentration to make sure you are getting the same amount and the same kind of facts on each property when you make your telephone inquiry.

The best way to both analyze ads and organize the information that results from them is to use a checklist. If you don't, you might conclude a detailed and instructive session with an agent on how you can buy the property with creative financing—and then, only after you have hung up, realize that you don't know how many bathrooms it has, whether it has parking or when you could obtain possession.

In preparing your checklist of specifications, put the most important ones on top. If you have already sold a house and need another quickly, when you can take possession should be one of your first questions. If you are severely limited in the amount of down payment you can pay and have no way to stretch it, the amount of the minimum down payment acceptable should be your number-one question.

Lovely, neat house, unique kitchen, extremely private patio, sunlit living room overlooking luxurious landscaping, 3BR. $180,000. Linda, XXX Realty, call 111-1111.

FACTS: kitchen, three bedrooms, living room, patio, $180,000 price.

PUFF: lovely, unique, neat, extremely private, sunlit, luxurious.

ANALYSIS: The puffery may be true, but you need more hard information to warrant making an appointment to inspect. A building can have a magnificent view yet be virtually uninhabitable. Lovely and unique vary greatly with the beholder. It's nice to have a sunlit living room, but if it is tiny, it's not worth much. There are enough clues here to suggest that this house is somehow out of the ordinary in a way that is not necessarily advantageous. It appears neither standard nor custom. Since the ad is so silent on size, that's one of the first things you should ask about.

WHAT YOU NEED TO KNOW: down payment, financing, square footage, number of bathrooms. "Neat" is sometimes a code word for small. Is there any yard other than the patio, and where is it?

OUTSTANDING FINANCING. 2BR, 2BA, patio home, never occupied. Vaulted ceiling, stained glass, skylights, French doors, formal dining. $102,000. Call Flora, XXX Realty 111-1111.

FACTS: never occupied, two bedrooms, two baths, probably a separate dining room, $102,000 price.

ANALYSIS: The location of this one is suspect. Real estate professionals are hyperaware of location. If it is anything to brag about at all, it always tops the ad.

Then there's the financing. Why doesn't the ad give some detail about what makes it so special—low down payment, lower than market interest rate, owner carryback without a balloon, or whatever?

The "never occupied" is a significant point. This means something different from new. The home could be a few months old or more. What is implied here is that it was sold once but the new owner never moved in. That could mean a variety of things: He immediately got transferred, he got disenchanted, he went in over his head, etc. It is a clue worth checking out.

When so much of the advertising dollar is given to touting the bells and whistles, as in this ad, one wonders about the size and the styling of the basic unit. Not all the features are that important or that desirable. Stained glass worth $100 hardly puts a unit in a different class. Skylights can be good or bad—charming when they are good, horrid when they are badly installed and leak rainwater. They can also make the house more expensive to heat and air-condition. Real vaulted ceilings denote a special house, but the phony kind—with prefabricated beams added after the fact or with the conventional ceiling omitted in favor of drywalling directly to the roof, without benefit of air space—can be a heating and cooling nightmare.

Keep a classified ad log. Organize the information into some kind of consistent filing system.

It's hard to go back and find an individual ad that intrigued you a few hours earlier among the hundreds in a fat section. If a few days or a few weeks have passed, forget it.

After you have circled the ads you like, you need to have them in a form that permits keeping your notes, from both telephoning and inspecting, tied to the ad.

If you have access to a photocopying machine, you can frame the circled ad by placing plain white paper over those ads you are not interested in, so that on the photoprint you will have plenty of white space to make notes. That may sound like a lot of fussing, but when you consider that going to look at a property is anything from a one- to three-hour commitment, any bit of organizing that saves you unnecessary running around is worth it.

Once you start collecting interesting ads in your notebook of photoprints, note the date each time it is advertised again.

Needless to say, once you start your looking process, you have to read the classified ads every day. Saturdays and Sundays are the most important, but you need to check the daily ads, too. You are more likely to find a sleeper in a midweek ad than on Sunday. The daily advertiser is often the advertiser in a hurry. It might be an estate closing, a forced sale, an impending foreclosure or just an amateur who isn't aware that Sunday is when the big bazaar appears. In any case, it is more likely to be a bargain than the house described with five inches of adjectives in the Sunday section.

Keeping track of properties advertised, even the ones you have looked at and turned down, is a good way of getting a feel for the market. If you observe that homes are selling within two weeks of being offered, or if you see that they hang around for months and go through a succession of changes in price or terms, you can better gauge what kind of market you are operating in.

* * *

After you have been following classified ads for a while, you will be able to penetrate the sales talk and spot offerings that sound good but aren't so interesting when you know the facts.

6

The Great Housing Flea Market

A home with a past or brand-new, a condo, a mobile?

You will have choices, a lot of them. Choosing among them can become hopelessly bewildering if you don't eliminate some at the outset.

In a metropolitan area of a million inhabitants, there could be 5,000 to 7,000 properties being offered at any one time. Of those there might be as many as 20 categories that you could identify: by price, by neighborhood, whether the homes are new or resales, by commuting distance, by school district, by your area preference, and so forth.

This is when your homework in planning your search will pay off. By narrowing the choices on paper, you can save yourself several weekends' worth of the physical labor of traipsing through all those buildings. The more you narrow your field of inquiry and the sharper the focus you get on it, the more likely you are to turn up a bargain.

The nature of your choices will be dictated largely by your geography. What classifies as a good buy in Yorba Linda might be exorbitant at the same price in Ypsilanti and totally unknown in Yonkers. The availability of land, the economic health of the area, the climate, the history and the ethnic heritage all influence both the size and the character of the housing inventory.

ARE YOU A COMMUTER?

The cost of land is the largest single variable in the price picture. Obviously, a builder can offer a larger housing unit for the same price in the relatively cheap land markets of Reading and Buffalo than he can in Washington, D.C., or San Francisco.

If you want to live the urban life—walk or be able to drive quickly to work, the fine restaurants, the concert halls, the libraries, the museums and the art galleries—you most likely will have to sacrifice space. That could mean living more compactly with fewer pieces of furniture. Sometimes it also means putting up with older or smaller shopping centers, particularly food stores.

If you demand room, lots of room, inside and out, you will have to commute for it. That's true not only of the very large city but also, increasingly, of the medium and smallish city, depending on how much growth in the form of new industry has come to it in recent years. In many areas even a willingness to live a good distance from the city won't necessarily mean you'll get the space you want.

Face the commuting issue head on. Know that if you insist on newness, you are not likely to find it in the city except in luxury custom and semicustom homes. That means the suburbs for you. How far into the suburbs depends on your budget. The more economical new houses are farther out, where the land is less expensive.

In some metropolitan areas new starter houses can be as much as 35 or even 50 miles out. One of the biggest mistakes beginning purchasers make in their house hunting is to go meandering instead of searching. They leisurely wander from one development to another, making plenty of stops in between. The farther out they go, the larger and more elaborate houses they see for the same price. By the time they find something that matches their original dream, they have wandered deep into commuterland, many miles from where they started and much farther out than they had considered living.

Then the "if only" agony starts: "If only this house were 20 miles closer, we would grab it in a minute." A wasted afternoon? It's more serious than that. Now they have to go 20 miles back to older and less glamorous houses, and the comedown is hard. Many a buyer turns down a plain house at a good price because he is still dreaming about the new one he would not buy. The irony is that this same buyer would be delighted to buy the same plain house weeks later after he has readjusted his sights and gotten back to reality. Chances are it won't be there waiting for him.

Do yourself a favor: Eliminate the if-only dilemma

by sticking to your territory. Aimless window-shopping not only doesn't solve problems, it creates them. Besides luring you into distant areas, unplanned shopping produces chaotic results. The shopper sounds like this: "I love the kitchen in the Muir Street house, but the Brown Avenue house is in a much nicer neighborhood. But on the other hand, the price on the Arcadia house is terrific," and on and on.

Some of this comparison of chicken and cheese is unavoidable, but it is a waste of time to collect ideal components, get stuck on them and then have to reject them because the neighborhood, style or price make the house unacceptable.

A low price range, for example, may limit your choices to condominium units. The word *condominium* does not always indicate economy—there are luxury condo units that fetch half a million dollars each—but in many markets condominiums are the least expensive of the alternatives facing the would-be homeowner. And even there you have to make a choice. Shall it be a brand-new, built-from-the-bottom-up condominium apartment on the edge of town? Or do you fancy a remodeled one in the heart of the city?

If you have already zeroed in on a location, it is possible that the choice of a new versus an existing house has already been dictated by that decision. This is especially true if you have chosen a close-in area. Few new houses are built in the older parts of the city except for an occasional speculative house or one built to an owner's specifications.

Assuming you do have a choice in the area you

want, what are the pros and cons of new and older houses? If you give up the new-house amenities (as builders now call everything from a community swimming pool to a built-in laundry chute), what are the trade-offs? The well-constructed new house has a longer physical life, certainly, but does that mean it is a better buy? What about the hidden costs, especially the unexpected ones, in an older house? Are all the pluses on the side of a new house? If not, what are the negatives?

NEW-HOUSE ADVANTAGES

Predictable cost. One of the reasons people like new homes is that once you make your down payment, you can be reasonably sure your monthly mortgage payment and your utilities are all you will have to spend for a few years to maintain the property.

Less maintenance. With all-new systems (plumbing, wiring, heating and air-conditioning) as well as all-new structural members (roof, weight-bearing beams, foundation) you can expect a minimum of repair and fix-up headaches for the first several years.

Modernity. You'll acquire the latest in the design of floor plans, kitchen and bathroom layouts, fixtures and appliances, plus the newest products in floor covering and window treatments.

Cheaper to furnish. Being able to choose the color of the wall-to-wall carpeting and perhaps blinds at all the windows can help reduce the decorating costs of settling in.

Energy efficiency. You can expect, though you cannot be positive, that a new house will be less expensive to heat and cool than a comparable older one.

Recreational features. Swimming pools, craft workshops and billiard rooms are frequently the dividends of living in large, new developments. Some have tennis courts, and a few remote ones have bridle paths.

Community atmosphere. In new developments there are often opportunities to participate in such things as entertainment, exercise programs, clubs and study groups.

NEW-HOUSE DISADVANTAGES

Location. Sometimes you can find a new house in a late phase of a close-in development, but in most markets the newer and larger the development, the farther out in the suburbs it is. With the ever-escalating cost of materials and the high cost of land and construction, builders are forced to build way out where they can still buy large enough tracts of land to accommodate a sizeable development.

Shoddy construction. Always a worry with some marginal builders, it has been increasingly worrisome in recent years, when many good builders have looked for ways to cut corners.

Smallness. To keep prices under control, builders are making homes smaller. An older home may give you more space for your money now that an increasing percentage of homes are less than 1,000 square feet.

The raw look. In all but the most expensive developments, the trees, foundation plantings and lawns are skimpy and the place looks barren. Furthermore, if a substantial part of the development has yet to be built, graded and paved, the nuisance and dirt can be considerable.

Look-alikes. Brick chimney, stone chimney; white shutters, brown shutters; garage on the left, garage on the right—those may be your only choices among the houses in a new development. You might like the consistency that look-alikes give to the character of a development. Or you might detest it, preferring to own a house with character of its own even if its neighbors are not your style.

Enforced togetherness. This factor is a joy to some, a pain to others. One builder conjectures that it is possible for people to want a new house without a built-in extended family. His ad reads: "No group walking! No group talking! No group swimming! No group singing! No group nuthin'!"

OLDER-HOUSE ADVANTAGES

Location. One thing many an older house has going for it over a new house is its established location near work, schools, shopping and transportation.

Size. Many older houses have larger rooms or more of them for the same price.

Individuality. If finding a house with character and maybe even a history of its own is important to you, you are an older-house buff.

Better construction. This is often but not necessarily true. It's something you have to check out on a case-by-case basis. Also, unless or until the older house is modernized, the new house has functional superiority.

Cheaper. The older house can be a better buy in real estate taxes. Because streets, sewers, schools and public utilities are already built, the tax rate may be less than in the newly developing areas where everything has to be built from scratch.

Mellower. Older trees and lawns and a variety of architectural styles as well as a range of color and texture of materials (brick, stone, wood, etc.) present a less monotonous, more seasoned and comfortable environment.

More flexible deals. When mortgage money is cheap, the new house is easier to buy, since lenders prefer to make commitments on new construction in large lots. When mortgage money is expensive, it is often easier to qualify for an older house and get a better interest rate if the seller is able to do all or part of the financing.

OLDER-HOUSE DISADVANTAGES

The uncertainty of the total cost. If the older house needs renovating, you can get reasonably close estimates of the cost. However, it is difficult to predict the exact timing for replacement of such items as a roof, a furnace, plumbing or a sewer.

Out-of-pocket costs. If you are planning on updating the kitchen or modernizing the bathroom, you might have to get a short-term home-improvement loan (which will drive up your monthly housing costs) or pay cash.

The temptation to overimprove. Many beginning older-house owners have to battle the urge to make them perfect. Knocking out that wall to create a larger living room, removing an exterior wall to put in more windows, enclosing porches, finishing the basement, adding a room—all may be desirable, but all are difficult and expensive.

SHOULD YOU CONSIDER CONDOMINIUMS?

First, a definition: *Condominium* is a legal term, not an architectural one. It describes a kind of ownership, not a kind of building or portion of a building. A condominium owner holds title to his unit just as he would with any other home, plus an ownership interest in the land and common areas. A unit may be an apartment, townhouse, detached house, beach house, office or warehouse.

CONDOMINIUM ADVANTAGES

Price. This is usually the condominium's chief advantage. A two-bedroom condominium apartment in the same area and general price category is almost always cheaper than a two-bedroom townhouse. Similarly, a two-bedroom condominium townhouse is substantially cheaper than a two-bedroom detached house.

Freedom from external maintenance. In many condo arrangements, you'll have no snow to shovel, no hedges to trim, no exterior painting, no roof repair, no cleaning of the gutters. But you'll have to pay for it, and that can be an increasingly expensive proposition.

Form of ownership superior to cooperatives. If you think that buying an apartment is the answer for you, you should note the advantages of condominium ownership over cooperative ownership. The most important single difference is the independence of ownership: You own your individual unit. In a cooperative you don't own the particular unit (although you have control over it). Instead, under the most common form of cooperative ownership, you hold shares in a corporation that owns the entire building.

This has a critical effect on the form of the financing. You can mortgage your condominium unit independently, exactly as though it were a house. With the cooperative unit you have to live with the blanket mortgage that covers all the units in a single loan. If you try to sell fairly early in your ownership, before you have paid much into the blanket mortgage, you won't face too much of a problem. If, however, you try to sell after you have been there for years and built up a considerable equity, your potential buyer may not be able to get enough money together to buy you out. Either he has to come up with all the cash or you have to take his note for whatever cash deficiency he may have.

If you are considering using an apartment as a stepping stone to a bigger property later, the inability to convert your equity to cash could be a considerable handicap. Also, having had a mortgage in your own name is a slightly stronger credit reference than having paid in on a group mortgage. It is easier to get mortgage number two when you can show that you have qualified earlier for mortgage number one and demonstrated a satisfactory payment record.

CONDOMINIUM DISADVANTAGES

Less freedom. Although a condominium has all the legal and tax advantages of regular homeownership, in most cases it means living in close proximity to your neighbors.

Most developments impose rules and regulations on what you can do to the exterior of your unit. Rules include such things as conforming to the color scheme and submitting to a standards enforcement committee the plans for any structural changes you wish to make. The development may either forbid the renting of your unit to a tenant or demand the right of approval of any prospective tenant. The development may also impose restrictions on selling your unit.

Unpredicability of monthly carrying charge. You will pay a monthly fee to your owners' association to run the condominium development. That generally includes garbage and trash collection, exterior maintenance, such as painting and paving, and the building of a reserve fund for emergencies. These fees can be anything from low to high, depending on the skill of the managers, the condition of the development, the services provided and the policy established by the board of directors. The trend in these charges in recent years has been up, not down. The real question is, Will they inch up or zoom up after you move in?

Politics. Whether you like organizational activity or not, you ought to participate in a certain amount of it to protect your interest. The condominium governing body (elected from the unit owners) manages the property held in common or hires someone else to do it. That means management decides whether to replace or repair the swimming pool motor, whether to resurface the private streets, whether to put a new roof on the apartment building.

Lack of privacy. Both the physical proximity and the need to be active in the governing group mean a somewhat less private life than is possible in a more traditional neighborhood, or even in a rental apartment in a high-rise building. When the same high-rise building turns condominium, the social chemistry changes. Instead of being disinterested tenants, everyone becomes an involved owner. The good side of that is there is more of a community spirit; the flip side, less privacy.

Hidden operating costs. Probably no single aspect of condominium ownership has occasioned so much outrage as the deliberate hiding by the builder of the true cost of running a project. A builder may secretly subsidize the operating costs in the first several months of the project to entice buyers with a modest monthly charge for upkeep. Once the project is sold out and the builder departs, the new owners are faced with the true costs. In some projects, this has meant doubling and even tripling of monthly charges. The outcry has occasioned the development of both public and private ombudsmen for condominium owners.

Reserve fund problems. Unless the committee of owners who run the project or the management they hire is setting aside adequate reserves for repairs and replacements, owners can find themselves saddled with a sudden large assessment for a new roof, road resurfacing or other work. If you're considering a condo, look for one that has adopted a financially conservative policy toward accumulating reserves rather than a policy of depending heavily on special assessments. Find out what assessments have been made during the past five years in addition to the regular condo fee. Obtain a summary of the physical condition of the building, including projections for major repairs.

LOOK AT TODAY'S MOBILE HOMES, TOO

The house that gets delivered to you on wheels has come a long way in recent years. According to a report of the President's Commission on Housing, almost 36% of all single-family homes sold in 1981— and the vast majority of those under $50,000—were mobile homes or, as the industry prefers to call them, manufactured homes.

Mobile homes first gained popularity as permanent residences with the retirement and resort crowd and with GIs returning home from World War II. Today they are an important source of affordable housing for the elderly, for first-time homebuyers, and for low- and moderate-income families.

A nationwide construction code that took effect in 1976 and is supervised by HUD has improved safety, quality and durability. In many cases mobile homes placed on permanent foundations have been holding their value and in some places have actually appreciated. The zoning restrictions and high land costs that kept mobile homes out of many desirable residential areas in the past have begun to change. Many specially designed parks are attractive and offer residents a community complete with swimming pools, recreation centers and nearby schools and shopping. Condominium mobile home developments allow residents to own part of the common facilities as well as their own units and lots.

While many conventional builders are downsizing their houses, mobile homes are getting larger. Single-wide mobile units can provide 900 to 1,000 square feet of space, and two or more single-wides can be joined to make double-wide, triple-wide or even larger combinations.

The industry says its homes sell for 25% to 50% less than comparable site-built homes, not counting the cost of buying the land or renting the site. An average-priced new unit costs about $19,500 and nearly always includes some furniture, major appliances, draperies and carpeting.

Most mobile homes are still financed with personal-property loans of 10 to 15 years, carrying interest rates one or two points above conventional home mortgage rates. Down payment is typically 20%.

FHA- and VA-backed loans are available, and in 1982 about 22% of all mobile homes were financed through those programs. The FHA insures 20-year loans up to $22,500 on single-wide units and $35,000 on double-wides. Loans on single-wides on a lot are insured to $35,000, double-wides to $47,500, for 25 years. The VA guarantee for mobiles is $20,000 or 50% of the loan, whichever is smaller, for 20 to 23 years. A home purchased with a VA guarantee may not require a down payment.

Some banks and savings and loan associations will also finance a mobile home with a conventional or FHA-insured mortgage loan of up to 30 years if the home is permanently set up on land or on land owned by the borrower.

7

The Truth About Location

Is it really all that important?

The old saw that the three most important things about a piece of real estate are (1) location, (2) location and (3) location may be a cliché, but like most clichés, it is true.

When an agent rushes into his real estate office excited about the hot new listing he has just obtained, the first question associates ask is not "How much?" or "How big?" but "Where is it?"

There is no single factor that affects the value of a home so much as location. It *does* matter which side of the tracks you are on when you go to sell or even to borrow on your home.

If you can't afford what you want *where* you want it, sacrifice something inside the house rather than sacrifice the location. You can make improvements, but you have to take what the neighborhood deals you. It is a poor trade-off to sacrifice location to get some feature that could be added, like a fireplace or a garage. The one thing you can't improve in your property is the location. If it is shaky, remote or in any way blighted, your property is less valuable no matter how fine a structure it may be. Better to take a house that needs a face-lift in a good neighborhood than to take one all dolled up in a marginal location at the same price.

The more likely you are to be putting your house on the market in a few years, the more attention you should pay to location. Even if you think you are going to be there forever, you should evaluate the neighborhood carefully for signs of change that could force you to move. Then, too, no matter what your plans are, you can never be sure when some emergency may force you to sell or to borrow against your equity. The better the location, the better the loan.

Obviously, everyone can't live behind the country club overlooking the seventh fairway—nor would everyone want to. Location, like many other values in a home, is a relative thing. A confirmed urban dweller and a confirmed suburbanite wouldn't dream of switching, yet both may be living in good locations.

A high price doesn't guarantee a fine location, either. There are good and bad $200,000 locations, just as there are good and bad $50,000 locations. Just because a builder elected to put a $200,000 house there doesn't make it a good location. Some builders, in an effort to fatten their profit margin, can't resist gambling on a cheap piece of land, often to their regret.

Trying to strike it rich by finding the fluke $70,000 home in a $200,000 neighborhood is all right for a hobby but not recommended for a serious home search. *Your goal should be to identify your price range first, find the best neighborhood in your area for that price range, and then pick the best home on the market within that neighborhood.*

SOUND LOCATION OR SOCIAL ADDRESS?

A property can be in a good location without its having the "right" address in the society sense. Some locations command premium prices far in excess of what the same house would command in another location. Beacon Hill in Boston, Nob Hill in San Francisco, Beverly Hills in Los Angeles, and Georgetown in Washington, D.C., are examples. All of these have fancy, quality homes, but they have a share of plain-Jane houses that command fabulous prices just because of where they are. These very expensive small or plain houses represent the ultimate example of the triumph of location over structure. Their tremendously inflated value is what professional appraisers call *caprice value*. The identical house a few miles away might command half the price.

Deliberately buying for caprice value is a perfectly sound investment. There is little risk in paying a premium for that kind of prestige address—provided that's the way you want to spend your money. Caprice value, if it is really established, not only holds up but grows. However, unless you can afford the top-quality houses in such a neighborhood, you will get much less house for the dollar—even to the point of discomfort—than you would get in a less fashionable area.

If you decide to buy for caprice value, make sure the high price is in line with the market for the area and not a gouger's price. Prestige areas often attract speculators who specialize in commanding wildly exorbitant prices. Getting a professional appraisal is an absolute must.

There is negative caprice value, too, which is not always discernible in a casual drive through an area. Just as some neighborhoods enjoy inflated values because the right people live there, others suffer a value deflated below what objective measurement would indicate because the right people wouldn't think of living there. If you are immume to that sort of social pressure, you can frequently find a very good value in one of those areas. Your profit might not be quite as great when you go to sell, but you will have a lot of livability in the meantime.

WHAT IS "LOCATION," ANYHOW?

Location as it affects the value of a home is its economic and social environment—its neighborhood. Defining a neighborhood isn't always easy. You can drift out of one and into another without being aware of it. The more defined a neighborhood is, the more likely the homes will maintain their value.

What you are looking for is a buffer of homogeneous properties and a stable social situation. An island of a few square blocks surrounded by blight or even much cheaper properties is normally not enough. A neighborhood has to have a dozen blocks or so and be contained within obvious boundaries to maintain a character of its own. A boundary can be a park, a major artery, a campus, a political boundary, a river, a string of stores—anything large enough to interrupt the pattern. A single boundary is better than nothing, but the more thoroughly a neighborhood is bounded, the better.

In a sprawling suburban setting a neighborhood might be as large as five square miles; in a city of well-defined neighborhoods it could be as small as six square blocks.

When it comes to affecting value, there is no such thing as a neutral neighborhood. Every neighborhood either adds to or detracts from the value of a property. The best way to get a feel for the importance of neighborhood is to imagine the same home in a number of different locations.

Pick a choice home in the poshest neighborhood of your city. Now mentally move it to the slum end of the city and take a guess at what it would be worth there. The effect is immediate and obvious. Putting a value on it would be an appraiser's nightmare because it would be unsalable there.

Next pick a setting that is a midway location, neither posh nor slum but a respectable, unfancy, working-class neighborhood, and install the posh house there. If you have an appraiser's eye for value, you will recognize that bringing it from a zero location to a middle neighborhood did not restore half of its value. If it was a million-dollar home in its original setting and a white elephant in its slum setting, the halfway location would not restore it to half its value, or $500,000. Nothing but a long and arduous sales campaign would determine its new value. It may not be a white elephant now, but it is still a difficult property to unload.

The moral of this tale is that a home must fit its surroundings. A poor fit imposes a harsh penalty on any home's value. What's true for the transplanted million-dollar home is just as true for a $75,000 house in a $35,000 neighborhood.

Compatibility is critical to value. Compatibility means that properties must be not only of the same class but also of the same type. A mix of single-family and multifamily properties can be detrimental to the single-family home. A mixture of densities and a broken skyline often indicate that as a single-family neighborhood this area is on the decline. For one thing, such symptoms could mean that the line on zoning has been broken. With the increase in density come parking problems and traffic.

A different sort of change lowers housing values in a neighborhood that's all apartment buildings to start with. There the beginning of blight takes the form of cheapening rents and a rash of "For Rent" signs. If the business district is encroaching and some of the apartment buildings are being renovated into office buildings, it may be a fine place to rent an office but a less-than-desirable place to buy a condominium apartment. More conversions to offices would mean an emptying out of the area at night and the eventual disappearance of food and convenience stores.

APPRAISING A NEIGHBORHOOD

Your appraisal of your future neighborhood should be every bit as thorough as your appraisal of the house itself. Chapter 9 discusses the importance of ordering an appraisal. A professional appraisal will reflect the appraiser's findings about the location, but don't settle for that in coming to your conclusion about the neighborhood. Appraisals, by their nature, deal in history, especially with the trend of sales as a barometer to a neighborhood's health.

You need to guess at the neighborhood's future. For that, you will have to engage in some rather unscientific but useful research. A neighborhood can be easing into a decline or starting into renewal before the sales figures reflect it. Give yourself time to analyze what's happening. Don't put it off until you are actually in negotiations over a particular home.

Shop the stores, noting the *kind* of stores and the *quality* of the merchandise. Nobody is as sensitive to subtle changes in the socioeconomic level of a neighborhood as the supermarket manager. Markets within the same chain stock their stores differently according to the neighborhood. The percentage of fancy goods and the percentage of more economical foods tell you a lot about whether it's a neighborhood you'd feel comfortable in.

Go to a community meeting of any kind: political, PTA, church, a zoning hearing, anything that will permit you to meet the residents and learn what their concerns are.

Go to the schools if you have children and meet the staffs.

Do at least one practice commute, no matter how early you have to get up to do it. Don't do it on a weekend and make a mental adjustment for a working day. You will be commuting a long time, so it's worth the effort to learn the truth. If you are planning on taking public transportation, try to determine whether there are any proposals to abandon that line.

SPOTTING BLIGHT

The easiest way to judge a neighborhood is to look for the negative factors first. After you have identified all the bad stuff, if any, you can better evaluate just how good the good is.

What you are looking for is blight and pollution. This doesn't mean doing a government-type study of the air quality, but you should eyeball and sniff the area for factors that reduce its desirability as a place to live.

Traffic. A heavy traffic flow is a major drawback in the single-family class of homes. Being on a busy street is less of a problem for a condominium apartment, but even there a unit on the quiet side of the building would certainly be more desirable than one where you can hear the steady whizz of traffic.

Poor upkeep. If there is a general atmosphere of neglect of both the structures and the yards, be careful. Full-blown blight is easy to spot. What you need to be alert to are the early signs before it has become obvious. Sometimes a neighborhood has the look of having been tip-top a few years ago. Nothing is broken, littered or really shabby, but it isn't ship-shape either. You need to find out why the level of maintenance has slipped. Often this is early evidence that a neighborhood is converting from one of owners to one of renters. If that is the case, and you like the house well enough to bid on it, your offer should reflect the fact that the neighborhood is less than prime.

Crowding. Summer is the best time to judge this. In cooler weather with everyone inside it is harder, but there are signs. If there seems to be an oversupply of cars for the area, so that streets and driveways are parked full, that's a bad sign. Some kinds of doubling up are worse than others. A neighborhood is more cheapened by the renting out of rooms than by any other sort of crowding. Next come the so-called light housekeeping units, which usually offer a makeshift kitchen of portable appliances and perhaps a shared bath.

Full-fledged apartments in single-family homes are all right if the remodeling and design are good. They don't add to a neighborhood, but they don't detract seriously, either.

Crime. The worst single blight an area can have is crime. Pass up the rumors and go to the police precinct station to get the hard evidence of what the rate of street crime and break-ins is for the area. Of particular importance: Is the rate going up or down?

Visual pollution. Look around for public utility substations and transformers, radio or television broadcasting towers, gas stations, auto dealerships, shopping centers, freeways, salvage yards, overnight parking for large commercial fleets, ball fields where night games are played.

Noise pollution. Visit the area at different times of day and night and on weekdays as well as weekends. Is it in the flight pattern for airplanes landing and taking off? Is it too close to a bus stop, a fire station or a school, particularly one with a large playing field?

Odor pollution. Does the commuting pattern create smog in the area? What about food-processing plants or other manufacturing, such as paper or metal factories. Even something that can be delightful in small doses, like the smell of bread wafting from a bakery, can become a nuisance when you can't escape it.

PICKING A FUTURE WINNER

Buying into an area that is strongly on the comeback trail can be an excellent investment if you do it right.

In an area of this kind, trend is everything. The trick is to not get in so early that you are one of the earliest pioneers but early enough that there is still plenty of appreciation left. Being an early pioneer is fine if you are a gambler possessed of lots of patience. It's safer, though, to buy into such an area after the restoration trend is unmistakably established. Don't be taken in by a few exterior face-lifts. To create real change, remodeling has to be thorough enough to put a house into new, or nearly new condition. And there must be a sufficient number of fully restored houses to create a new atmosphere.

A neighborhood that's a good candidate for restoration has to have an intrinsic location advantage: It must be next to a prestigious area, say, or in a good walk-to-work location or next to an important park. It must also have good basic houses. They can be in a woefully dreary state after years of rooming-house service, but they have to have been quality structures of some architectural merit originally.

AVOIDING A FUTURE LOSER

Don't think that just because you don't see any blight, you are home free. Many times it is even more important to check on what you can't see: future developments. A neighborhood can look peaceful and inviting when you buy into it and a month later be a construction disaster area with the building of a new outer loop, inner loop, beltway, access road or whatever. A visit with key officials at the city hall or courthouse or with members of the city council or board of supervisors could save you from a miserable mistake.

Several kinds of public decisions could affect your future neighborhood. Here are some of them:

Highway construction and street pattern changes. An overpass can have a major effect on surrounding property. Plans to make a street one-way for faster commuting or to restrict parking may indicate an increase in congestion.

Zoning changes. One stroke of the pen at city hall can change the whole character of a neighborhood. If you are wondering why such a nice home is on the market at such a favorable price, maybe the seller knows something you don't. Find out whether the city fathers have made or are contemplating a zoning change that would permit a high-rise apartment complex or an office building overshadowing you.

A change of use for a large institution. Converting a boarding school for girls to a trade school could make a real difference. The closing of any school or college poses a problem to a neighborhood. Unless the school is standing on valuable commercial ground that would make it salable, it often becomes an eyesore and a target for vandalism. And if it is sold, the land may become the site of warehouses, not homes.

Private builders' plans. If you buy into a neighborhood of open vistas with large lots and a huge vacant tract across the street and six months later the concrete trucks roll in to start construction on 100 townhouses on that vacant tract, you're going to be sick. It's harder to learn about private building plans than public ones unless they are fairly well along. Once they've reached the building permit stage, you can find what the plans call for by inquiring at your city or county building permit office. If the land is being offered for sale, you are on notice that change is on its way. If it isn't posted for sale, and that vista is critical to your decision to buy, you would be wise to learn the owner's name from the city assessor's office and call him. Chat with the zoning officials about whether there have been any applications for a rezoning and the kind of rezoning request they would entertain.

It can happen to you in an urban setting, too. Just

because the area you pick has no obvious buildable land in sight doesn't mean you are safe from change. Small, old houses or stores are favorite targets of in-town builders, particularly if they can string enough of them together to assemble a plot for an apartment building or a cluster of townhouses. Zoning, both present and potential, is the key. The philosophy of your zoning officials and the presence or lack of a master plan determine an area's future for increased density. Depending on the builder and the price range he plans, the new development of townhomes might be an improvement.

If you are considering a suburb well out from the city, look for coming freeways, beltways, industrial parks and huge shopping centers that would be too close.

CHANGES FROM THE OUTSIDE

Every neighborhood changes. Even the apparently rock-ribbed stable neighborhood changes, however slowly. Typical of such a shift is the once-remote country club district that is now a green island in a sea of pavement because the city has grown up to surround it. The 100 houses within are still grand, but there is a different crowd living in them, and the homes no longer command a price commensurate with their size and quality.

An intown neighborhood can be affected by the growth of the suburbs into areas not served by public transportation. Forced to drive their cars partway at least, the commuters drive as far into the city as they can and still park free. They clutter up endless side streets along a bus route with their all-day parking.

You can suffer parking pollution on the edge of the city, too, if yours is a convenient neighborhood for employees to walk to their jobs in a shopping center or office park.

In picking a neighborhood, you obviously can't predict all the possibilities, but with a little diligence you can spot the near-term probabilities. The time you take to do that could be the most valuable time spent on your home search.

8

Broker, Agent, Realtor

Who's who?

Imagine a hospital where every level of staffer was called doctor—the nurse, the orderly, the lab technician, the therapist, even the janitor. It's doubtful that the word *doctor* would conjure up the feeling of confidence and trust that it does now.

That's a little like what has happened in real estate. No matter how high or low the skill, no matter whether the training is limited to an examination-prepping mill or extends to a doctorate or M.B.A. from a major business school, there are only two titles in the business, and the public sees precious little difference. They are broker and agent.

A broker is someone licensed by the state and permitted to conduct a real estate business and to negotiate transactions for a fee. An agent is a broker's sales employee; the state says he—or, more often, she—can sell real estate provided he is employed by a licensed broker. Both can properly be called agents because they act as agents for their clients.

A broker may or may not be a Realtor; an agent may or may not be a Realtor Associate. Public per-

ception and media usage notwithstanding, the word
realtor written with a small *r* is incorrect. A Realtor
and a Realtor Associate (who works for a Realtor) are
members of the National Association of Realtors, a
trade organization. According to the association, its
members account for about 85% of all active, licensed real estate personnel. Realtists are members
of the National Association of Real Estate Brokers, a
smaller national group.

THE COMPETENCY QUESTION

In most states an individual is permitted to call
himself an agent after taking a required amount of
classroom instruction and passing a state examination preliminary to being licensed. (A few states have
no educational requirements.) An agent must work
for a broker. After taking roughly double the classroom hours and usually acquiring at least a year's
experience, an agent can sit for a more difficult
examination and become a broker.

Many leaders in the real estate industry have
worked long and valiantly to make their field more
professional, but its entrance requirements remain
low. All too often any literate person who has the
money and concentration sufficient to take some
classes and pass an examination is in.

Staying in is another matter. Agents leave in
droves, either disappointed or disenchanted, but
there is always a new crop coming in to take their
place. Many don't stay long enough to become really
professional. In the 1981 profile of agent members the

National Association of Realtors found that nearly 65% have five years or less in the business and 31% are part-timers.

Many industry leaders contend that the business has become too complicated for a part-timer to make the grade. Some larger firms won't even hire them, but the fact remains that there are brokers who welcome new part-time agents in the front door as they show the failed ones the back door.

There is no nationally recognized or prescribed sequence of university-level study for real estate. In fact, most states require fewer classroom hours to qualify for taking the real estate examination than they do for hairdressers.

The standard for brokers is substantially higher. A total of 45 to 90 classroom (not semester) hours is the usual requirement. The toughest state is Texas, which demands 720 hours, but it allows related subjects, such as accounting, management or business, to count toward the requirement. The majority of states require fewer than 100 hours.

All of this is said to alert you to the importance of finding an experienced agent who works for a well-respected broker.

FINDING AN AGENT

You can't move around in the home-buying scene very long without encountering agents. Unless you make a determined effort to avoid it, you probably will end up dealing with one. Whether that proves to be a profitable and pleasant experience or an exercise in frustration depends on two things:

• The agent's level of professionalism.
• How clear you are about what you want and what you can afford.

You have a choice at the outset: Either you can wander around on your own meeting agents at open houses or on appointments as you respond to their ads, or you can choose one to be your scout.

There's good and bad to both approaches. As a practical matter, it's a good idea to shop the field first and then pick an agent. If a friend has had good luck with an agent, that can be the very best way to find one.

By sticking with the potluck approach, you may get exposure to more properties (assuming your search is a particularly energetic one), but this approach will get you the least service. You will encounter a succession of agents, and their relationship to you will be exactly that of department store clerk to purchaser: They'll write up your order if you want to buy the merchandise at hand, but they won't go out looking for you.

If you stick with a particular agent, assuming you choose well, you can expect more service. How much service depends totally on the selling style of the individual agent.

Agents generally take one of two distinct approaches to selling: One sticks with a particular property and waits for the right buyer to come along;

the other meets a buyer who wants service and makes an effort to find the right home for him, weeding out places he wouldn't be interested in, making suggestions and giving advice.

There is a widespread misunderstanding about the purchaser-agent relationship. Unless specifically hired for a fee by the buyer, the agent performs as the agent of the seller. The seller pays the commission, making the seller-broker (and by delegation, seller-agent) relationship a fiduciary one. Most agents work on a strictly commission basis, although some large firms put their agents on a base salary and pay some commission on top of that. By law commissions are negotiable. In practice they are most often negotiated at 6% to 7% or close to it.

Even when you pick an agent, that agent isn't really your agent in the sense that he or she owes you any time, any service or even results. It is not an employer-employee relationship as it is with the seller. Rather it is a noncontractual, informal relationship between two parties, both of whom are gambling. The agent is gambling his time that you will remain loyal and do your buying through him. You are gambling that in return for your loyalty to that agent, he will produce both a property and a quality of service that will make that loyalty rewarding.

YOU CAN ALSO HIRE A BUYER-AGENT

When the market is brisk, it may be hard to find an agent to give you any special time. If you are a buyer with limited time to shop or particular needs, or if you would like to be assured that you have the system working for you, consider hiring a buyer's agent. That way you ensure that you have a real estate professional working on your side.

This is a new field in residential real estate, but an old one in commercial real estate, where sophisticated buyers often insist on having their own representative. Few real estate firms offer this service, although any licensed broker may act as a buyer's agent.

When you hire a buyer-agent, you enter into a contract for service. It may involve a fee up front or an hourly fee.

In exchange your buyer agent will not only look for you specifically but also negotiate for you. The agent's fee represents an additional cost for your house hunt, but a good agent will earn the fee by saving you time and negotiating a better price than you might be able to get on your own.

Before you commit yourself to this kind of relationship, find out what the fee will be and how it is calculated, and make sure everything is spelled out in the contract. Is there a minimum charge regardless of how little time it takes to find a home? How long does the contract stay in force? What will happen if you buy a home without the buyer-broker's help during the contract period? Does your contract state in writing what steps will be followed in the event of a dispute?

An agent has to have well-developed skills in bird-dogging and negotiating to be of any use to you as a buyer's agent. Whether you are picking a seller's agent to act as your unpaid scout or buyer's agent to act as your paid representative, there are certain signs to look for.

WHAT TO LOOK FOR IN AN AGENT

If location, location, location are the watchwords for picking a property, experience, experience, experience are the watchwords for picking an agent. This is particularly true if you are thinking of hiring a buyer's agent.

Before you decide to spend much time with an agent or rely on him as a finder, interview him. The agent is going to qualify you, and a good one will qualify you pretty thoroughly before he decides to spend much time with you. He will want to know whether you can afford what you say you want and how much you know about what you want. That's a good sign. If you meet an agent who seems to be willing to devote all kinds of time to your project without knowing much about you, drop him—he's an amateur.

When your agent gets done qualifying you, qualify him. Ask how many years he has been selling and for whom. Look for an agent with a track record for selling. The recent past makes a good test for effective agents, so find out whether your agent weathered the real estate depression of the early '80s with the sale of real estate as his main support.

HOW TO PICK A BROKER

As a practical matter the buyer spends most of his shopping time with an agent rather than the broker unless he is dealing with a small, independent broker who does his own selling. Most buyers don't chose a broker; they acquire one after meeting his sales employee, the agent, at an open house or by responding by telephone to an ad or a "For Sale" sign. There is nothing wrong with that for starters, but before you spend much time or place your dependence on an agent's ability to fill your special requirements, you should take a look at the firm he works for. An agent can't rise above his broker, so it's the broker's reputation in the industry and the community that you should look at.

For the house hunt, it's the individual agent's intelligence, integrity, resourcefulness and intuition that count most heavily. But when you've found the house, what counts is the broker's expertise with contracts and negotiating, how much other brokers are willing to cooperate with him, his influence with lenders, and his skill and experience in solving the knotty problems that can suddenly appear and threaten a deal at a late hour. You want to be sure that if the agent you are dealing with doesn't have the technical know-how, he is backed up by a broker who does.

How then to judge a broker's know-how? One way is to ask your friends, acquaintances, associates and relatives who have bought homes recently for recommendations. The best question to put is, "If you had to buy a home tomorrow, would you use the same broker?''

Another good technique is to ask your prospective neighbors. Go into the area where you think you'd like to buy a house, knock on doors and find recent purchasers. Ask them whom they dealt with and how they liked their treatment. With this approach you will get a broker who is active in the area you want, which may not be true of referrals you get from your friends.

9

You Found It! Should You Grab It?

Not until you've sought professional *advice*

After what has seemed like endless hours of traipsing through all kinds of houses, you've finally found a house you think is right for you.

You may be tempted to grab it immediately, or you may go to the other extreme and freeze with apprehension at making such a major decision. Either way, this is the time to seek advice.

If you've had experience buying houses and feel competent to judge them yourself—or if you are offering enough below the market price to leave yourself room to absorb surprises like a bad roof or a furnace heading toward its last season—you could skip getting professional advice. But you would definitely be taking a risk.

Most buyers are better off having the building checked out by a professional engineer, contractor or inspection service. They should probably also have the price tested by an appraiser or a disinterested broker.

But before you spend one thin dime on advice, make sure you are ready for it. You should be at the stage where you can say to yourself, "I have pretty much decided to buy this house *if* it checks out."

If your attitude is more like, "I *might* be interested. Let's see what the experts say," save your money. You are not ready.

Much of the advice that buyers seek does them more harm than good either because it is not professional or because it comes from a professional who is volunteering advice outside his specialty.

It can be a serious mistake to take the advice of a layman, whether he is a relative, a friend or the fellow at the office who owns a couple of rental houses. Relying on amateur advisers is often a clue that you don't want advice so much as you want someone to talk you in or out of a deal.

The most common difficulty with amateur advice is that it is based on ignorance. Amateurs base their judgments of your purchase by comparing it with their own, whether it fits or not. The friend who bought a house a few years ago—or even a year ago— is not an expert on the right price for your house even if it is in the same neighborhood. He bought in a different market and may or may not have gotten a good deal for himself. The friend who bought one last week in a different part of the city is not a reliable guide, either. The business associate who paneled his own den doesn't qualify as a structural expert capable of telling you whether your house is sound.

USING A PRO

If you hire a professional, make sure you listen to him only about his own field: appraisers on value, contractors on structure, lawyers on contract language.

Don't hire anyone without asking his fee. Fees differ widely among the specialties and from one locale to another. No matter where you are, you will pay a little more for a written opinion than an oral one, but it's worth it. Any adviser is more careful about a written opinion.

Advisers won't push you over the line if you're hesitating. If anything, advice tends to pile up on the negative side. Some advisers, if they sense you are wobbling, will be very negative because they feel you want them to take you off the hook. So take yourself off the hook and save your money. Keep on looking.

Advice can actually add to indecision. *No professional adviser can be expected to father you into a safe decision, nor even to offer encouragement.* An adviser's function is to dispense information, not enthusiasm. It is well to be aware, however, of a certain type of advice giver who, under the guise of extreme care, regularly dispenses discouragement. This sort seems to feel that he makes his greatest contribution by pointing with alarm. This may spring from a naturally cautious disposition, but often it is a determined avoidance of future involvement. Such an adviser figures that you won't come crying to him a year later about the purchase you did not make, but you might well come complaining about the one you did make. The ultracautious adviser is protecting himself against ever having to listen to you say, "I wish you had talked me out of it."

WHAT KIND OF ADVICE SHOULD YOU SEEK?

Price. The agent or seller should have provided you with a market analysis showing what similar properties sold for recently. If this seems complete, if there are enough recent comparable sales, if you have looked enough in that neighborhood to have an informed opinion, you may be comfortable without outside advice on price. If not, or if the selling circumstances are unusual—such as an estate sale or court-ordered sale—or the property has been on the market unusually long, has an expensive addition or is underdeveloped relative to its neighbors, it is wise to get an appraisal. An appraisal can also be a useful bargaining tool when you negotiate price with the seller.

You can hire a disinterested real estate broker or a professional appraiser. If you decide on an appraiser, pick one who specializes in residential appraisals. If you expect to finance your purchase through a commercial lender, the best place to start looking for an appraiser is with a lender. Pick one he recommends; that way, there's a good chance he will accept the appraisal for financing purposes. Before a lender will make you a loan, he will order an appraisal. *If you choose an appraiser who is not on the lender's list, no matter how well credentialed, there may have to be a second appraisal later.*

There are two prestigious organizations of real estate appraisers, both of which require rigorous training and an internship:

• The American Institute of Real Estate Appraisers, 430 N. Michigan Ave., Chicago, Ill. 60611. Your local Board of Realtors will have a list of members.
• The Society of Real Estate Appraisers, 645 N. Michigan Ave., Chicago, Ill. 60611. This organization has chapters in every state and many cities.

Appraisals are done in varying degrees of complexity. Before you hire an appraiser, tell him exactly what the purpose of the appraisal is and ask about his fee. One appraisal report commonly used by lenders is written on a standard FNMA form. Depending on where you live, this sort of appraisal may run anywhere from $150 to $350 and should include a list of limiting conditions, pictures of the house and street, a map locating the site and possibly a floor plan.

A more complex appraisal, the full narrative report, is rarely needed in a routine home purchase and is much more expensive. This kind of appraisal is frequently required for such purposes as court testimony or to settle an estate, and it may run well over 100 pages.

You cannot use an FNMA report for a VA or FHA purchase, and you cannot use a VA or FHA appraisal for a conventional loan. Usually a seller who is amenable to VA or FHA financing—and you can't get it if he is not—will have already obtained a conditional commitment or a certificate of reasonable value from the VA and FHA. Their appraisals are interchangeable.

Structure and mechanical systems. The professional adviser you use to evaluate the physical aspects of your prospective purchase could be a carpenter, contractor, building consultant or someone from a commercial company. Be wary, though, of advice from anyone who stands to benefit from work you'll be contracting for at a later date.

In major cities you can usually find inspectors listed in the Yellow Pages under "Building Inspection Services." Anyone who wants to do so can advertise himself as an inspector, so ask for recommendations and check qualifications and professional affiliations. Members of the American Society of Home Inspectors, for example, must pass a comprehensive entrance examination, complete 1,000 paid home inspections (or meet additional education requirements and complete 400 paid inspections) and agree to participate in continuing education classes.

No matter whom you call in, you should expect the inspection to take one to two hours. Many inspectors encourage buyers to accompany them, but you should also get a written report covering the major structural elements inside and outside the house; the capacity of the heating and cooling systems in relation to the size of the house; information on the age of the systems, their normal life expectancy and the condition and adequacy of the electrical wiring and plumbing, plus notes on appliances, repairs and additions that may be needed soon. Basements, crawl spaces and attics should be thoroughly examined and comments made on moisture, ventilation, insulation and construction. Outside, the condition of the roof, gutters, downspouts, drainage, siding, caulking and paint should be checked and the extent of impending repairs noted.

If you are considering a used home covered by a home warranty program offered either by the seller or the broker, don't assume that this eliminates the need for inspection. All that's offered by the typical warranty program, such as American Home Shield or Ticor Home Protection, is the guarantee that it will keep certain specified mechanical equipment operating for a year after you buy. The seller usually buys the warranty, but you will be responsible for paying a fixed service fee if anything goes wrong during that period. *The warranty is not in any sense an assurance that the equipment is in good condition.* In fact, none of the major firms offering warranty services actually inspect the property. A warranty service won't tell you whether a home is well or cheaply built. It won't tell you whether the home is underwired or whether the plumbing is in its last stages.

If the home you're considering is new, it may be covered by a Home Owners Warranty. HOW provides ten years of protection against faulty construction, backed by insurance, and the HOW coverage remains with the house if it is sold within those ten years. If a builder refuses to fix his mistake, insurance covers the repairs. A built-in dispute-settling process determines the outcome when buyer and builder disagree.

The builder pays a fee to get a HOW policy on the

house, and he usually passes it along to the buyer in the selling price. A buyer of a $100,000 home could expect to find $220 to $500 added to the price to cover the HOW.

During the first year, HOW builders warrant their new homes to be free from defects in workmanship and materials, major structural defects and flaws in the electrical, plumbing, heating, cooling, ventilating and mechanical systems. They guarantee the same items during the second year of the policy with exception of workmanship and materials. In the remaining eight years of HOW protection, the home is covered against major structural defects by the insurance feature alone.

Some very respectable builders do not choose to belong to HOW. Some offer their own warranty program. The next few years will doubtless see a proliferation of home warranty programs as more builders decide to offer their own and other national and local programs competitive with HOW develop.

In evaluating any warranty program offered you, check it out first with your state insurance commissioner to see whether that office has any information on it. Also make sure it has some provision for an arbitration procedure; without that it is more of a good-faith promise than a true warranty.

EVALUATE THE ADVICE YOU GET

When you get a professional report on a house, the first thing to do is decide whether there is anything in it to warn you off that particular home completely. (Example: The appraiser tells you the contract price is in line with the market but points out that the price trend for this neighborhood has been declining steadily in recent years. Or he finds a serious structural defect.)

Once you've decided that there is nothing wrong with the property that the right price can't cure (remember, there is *something* undesirable about every property), then it becomes a matter of how much you should pay, when you should offer it, and what strings you should attach to your offer. All of these decisions are strategic ones and so are part of negotiating. Now comes the test to see whether you can get what you want at the price you want to pay. You are ready to negotiate.

10

Wangling the Best Deal for Yourself

Know what you want

Every signal you send your seller, either directly or through his agent, about what sort of buyer you are is a part of the bargaining process. Everything you can learn about the seller, particularly about his reason for selling, is also part of the process.

How well you will fare in your negotiations with him depends greatly on how serious he is about selling. Maybe the seller is leaving town, is getting divorced, has already bought a new home with a deadline for settling on it, has suffered a business reversal or has developed a health problem. The more you can learn about his reason for selling, the better your chances of driving a good bargain. It's hard to get a good deal out of a seller who is just fishing for a price that assures him a certain profit and is content to stay put if he doesn't get it.

THE PSYCHOLOGY OF NEGOTIATING

Your preliminary bargaining begins the first day you walk into the property. It includes your attitude, what you tell about yourself and what you learn about the seller. The best posture is to be friendly but demand specific information. If you ask about the capacity of the water heater, don't accept "I don't know, but we never run out" as an answer.

Going back to look at the home two, three or even more times is good strategy. Don't be afraid to let the seller know you are interested, but make sure he gets the impression that you are a careful buyer. Bringing in such professionals as an appraiser and a building contractor is not only a good precaution, it is also an excellent bargaining device because if you do make an offer below the asking price, you have some objective justification for it. An appraisal from a respected professional is a more effective bargaining weapon than hours of argument from you, either directly, or through the agent. The seller can always dismiss your opinion of value as being self-serving, and perhaps uninformed. It's much harder to talk down an objective, professional opinion.

It is also important to impress your agent with your stance as a thrifty buyer. Remember, the agent normally acts for the seller and is obligated to get the best deal for him. Whether you should make your final offer on price right away or send up a trial balloon in the form of a lesser offer depends on how brisk the market is, particularly the market for that house. If you decide to try for a lower figure first, don't let the agent know that you might be willing to go higher, because if the seller then asked his agent directly whether he thought you would go higher, the agent would be obliged to tell him, yes, there is a chance of getting a higher price.

Price is important, but it isn't everything. Rank the several elements in the deal according to their importance to you: price, financing, date of possession, extras, time to have the property analyzed. That will be important when you are faced with a counter offer from the seller. A price reduction of several hundred or a thousand dollars is more important than having the bedroom draperies included. You probably won't get everything you want, so it is a good idea to decide in advance what you are willing to give up in exchange for something you really want.

Good negotiating has more to do with knowing exactly what you want from a deal than it does with playing tough bargainer. As a practical matter, you probably won't be doing your own negotiating if you're dealing through an agent, as most buyers do.

Inexperienced buyers are probably more handicapped by their ignorance about negotiating than any other single aspect of the whole complicated real estate transaction. Many buyers don't know they can bargain, and many agents won't tell them. *As a buyer, you have to be the one who initiates the bargaining.* A good agent will do a thorough job of presenting your list of demands if you name them. This is where an agent's experience really counts. If you lack confidence in the agent's ability, ask to have your contract presented by the broker.

YOUR OFFER IN WRITING

A purchase offer can become a binding agreement on both you and the seller. It is no less a contract if it is called an offer, binder or earnest money agreement or if it spells out only the terms of the sale.

Since a real estate contract is generally assumed to be all-inclusive, everything of importance should be written into it. Your contract should include the sales price, down payment, description of the property and any other items being sold with the home; the way title is to be conveyed to you; the fees to be paid and who will pay them; the amount of deposit; the conditions under which the seller and buyer can void the contract; the settlement date; how financing will be arranged; and so on.

It's a good idea to arrange for a real estate attorney before you reach the point of making an offer on a home. If you don't know a good real estate attorney, get names from your lender, title company and broker and get recommendations from friends. Because of the increasing complexity of home buying, it is important to get an experienced attorney. If you are buying a condo, co-op or farm, try to find a lawyer who specializes in that particular type of transaction.

Everything that goes into a contract, including the contract form itself, is subject to negotiation. It's a good idea to familiarize yourself and your attorney with the contract to be used by the agent before it comes to contract writing time. Get contingencies you plan on using (such as those for property inspection and attorney review) drawn up or approved by your attorney.

When you are ready to make an offer, either have the attorney draw up the contract or make sure there is a clause in the contract making it contingent on a review by him. This and other common contingency clauses and additions are usually not found in most preprinted contract forms, so you must ask to have those you want inserted. All additions to a contract must be signed by you and the seller in order to be valid. You can also arrange to bring the contract prepared by your agent to your attorney *before* it is presented to the seller, but it may be more practical to have the contingency clause.

WHAT'S IN THE CONTRACT?

Form and amount of the deposit. This is where money really talks. You can't make an offer and expect to get an answer that you can hold the seller to unless you make a firm offer backed by an earnest money deposit. In fact, the less bargaining you do verbally, the better.

It's poor strategy to let the other side know what you are going to do until you are ready to do it. Don't telegraph your thinking without learning theirs. Sophisticated sellers (or sellers advised by sophisticated brokers) virtually never bargain verbally. Their reasoning is that it pays to keep personalities out of the negotiating process and it never pays to cut one's price except for a ready, willing and able buyer. A contract backed by a deposit puts you in that class.

The agent will ask for a check. If you don't have sufficient funds in your checking account, he may take a personal note and require that you replace it with a check in a few days. The amount of deposit varies with local custom. In some areas it may run as much as 5% or even 10% of the sales price. If the broker doesn't routinely deposit earnest money in a trust account or with a neutral third party, such as a title company, escrow service or attorney acting as an escrow agent, have that requirement added to your contract.

Such a clause is doubly important if you are dealing directly with an individual seller. Never make out a deposit check to a seller. Put it in the hands of a neutral third party, an attorney mutually acceptable to both parties, a title company or an escrow company—whoever may be handling the final closing for you. Private individuals are not answerable to any regulatory authority as to how they handle funds while a deal is pending. You might have to sue to get your money back. You may also want to protect yourself in case the deal falls through by specifying in the deposit-refund clause that your money will be returned within a fixed time period after the contract is voided.

You should be aware that if you change your mind after your contract offer is accepted and signed by the seller, you could legally lose your deposit and even be liable for damages. Likewise, if the seller simply backs down—a very unusual occurrence—you can sue for damages or try to enforce the contract.

If the seller doesn't accept your offer, or if he

accepts and is then unable to meet a condition in the contract (by giving you a "good" title, for instance), your deposit should be returned. If the offer is accepted and signed, the deposit is placed in an escrow account until closing, when it is normally credited as part of your down payment.

Size of the down payment. This is directly affected by what financing you get. That's why it is so important to have a talk with a lender early in the game. When you do see something you want to negotiate for, you will then have an idea what your bargaining strength is.

If you are sure of getting financing from a commercial lender, the seller probably doesn't care how much your down payment is. It's an all-cash deal to him, whether the money comes from your pocket or out of the lender's. In any case, your contract should indicate that if you can't obtain a written loan commitment within a specified time, and at the terms agreed on, the contract will become void and your deposit will be returned in full.

This clause gives you the best of both worlds: You take the property off the market so it can't be bought out from under you, and at the same time you have an opportunity to shop for financing for this particular home. Getting a loan commitment is a double-hurdled job. You must pass muster as a borrower, and the home must be approved for the mortgage you want to place on it.

If you are asking for seller financing, you have more flexibility with the down payment than you would have on a commercial loan, in which you have to meet the lender's requirements. With seller financing the down payment can be anything you and the seller agree to.

If you are short of cash, you could try offering the down payment in installments over a period agreeable to the seller. How much luck you will have with that will likely depend on how much competition you have from more liquid buyers.

Whatever creative financing you use, be absolutely sure you understand what you are agreeing to. Some techniques, such as short-term balloon loans and contracts, are more risky than others.

Date of possession. This can be an important bargaining chip in cases where either party has deadlines to be met. If your seller is leaving the city or waiting for a new home to be completed, you might gain other concessions that are important to you by allowing him to stay longer than the usual time. Such agreements can have unexpected legal and tax consequences, so the documents should be written by an attorney and carefully examined before being accepted. Obviously, you'll have to decide whether the trade-off is worth it, but sometimes sellers are willing to make substantial concessions by lowering the price or throwing in extras when they have a difficult moving situation.

Time limit on your offer. Your contract should require the seller to accept your offer in writing by a certain date, say within two days. If you fail to specify this, you invite having your contract "shopped." That means that the seller or agent may use your offer to stimulate slower-moving buyers to top your offer. There is something in the psychology of buyers that makes them want to move quickly on a property they may have been dallying with when they hear that someone else wants it.

The fine print. Never make assumptions about what is in a printed contract. Brokers, attorneys and developers usually have printed versions of frequently used contracts available, but they vary tremendously. Read every word in every paragraph of any contract you are considering. Remember, you aren't obligated to use a broker's or builder's standard contract. You are free to present your offer on a contract that has been prepared to meet your particular requirements, but expect the seller to insert the conventional safeguards for himself if the contract you offer fails to do so.

The extras. Custom varies from one locality to another as to whether stove, refrigerator, washer and dryer are items regularly included in the sale or are considered personal property. Never take for granted that they are included if that is not specifically stated in the contract. Sometimes a seller will stick to a price as a point of pride but throw in several thousand dollars' worth of appliances, draperies and even rugs. If that happens, be careful that you aren't indirectly paying new-merchandise prices for items that have seen their best days.

Time to inspect. When you make an offer, put in a clause that gives you not only time to have the property inspected but also an out if the property doesn't pass satisfactorily. Normally, you won't be granted a lot of time because sellers and brokers alike regard this as a large loophole and are reluctant to take the property off the market for long. They are also alert to the fact that a buyer with second thoughts may use the report to get out of the deal. Don't be surprised if your seller insists that the inspection be done within a week by a recognized professional and that he receive a copy of the report without cost.

You will enhance your chances of getting this clause accepted if you have your inspection team lined up to move on short notice.

A critical portion of a typical inspection clause reads: "This contract is contingent on a property inspection report which, in the sole judgment of the purchaser, is deemed satisfactory . . ." You can see that a contingency clause with that kind of wording leaves a loophole as big as the house itself. To get the clause in, you may have to stress that you are very interested in the house and point out your willingness to spend the $150 or so that a good inspection will cost.

Termite inspection. Many contracts today require the seller to order and pay for a termite inspection. If such a clause is not in yours, put it in.

11

Getting a Good Title

Without it, your dream home could be a nightmare

When you buy a home, you are essentially buying the seller's title—his right to own, possess, use, control and dispose of his property. The written legal evidence that his ownership rights have been conveyed to you is a properly executed and recorded deed. Naturally, you want a deed that gives you the most assurances and rights to your new property and promises you a marketable title, one you can in turn convey to someone else. At closing time you want to feel sure that the title you're getting is what you expected and what it is represented to be.

There are three basic methods of assuring everyone concerned that a title is good.

Title insurance. This is the predominant method of protection in Alabama, Alaska, Arizona, California, Connecticut, Florida, Hawaii, Idaho, Illinois, Indiana, Kansas, Maryland, Michigan, Missouri, Montana, Nevada, New Jersey, New York, North Carolina, Ohio, Oregon, parts of Pennsylvania, Rhode

Island, South Carolina, Texas, Utah, Virginia and Washington.

Before the insurance is issued, a title report is prepared, based on a search of the public records. The report gives a description of the property and shows the owner, title defects, liens or encumbrances of record. Following examination of the title, the company will normally insure the title. If problems are discovered, the company can still insure by requiring that certain conditions be met or by making the insurance coverage subject to certain specified exceptions.

Abstract plus an attorney's opinion. This method is widely used in Arkansas, Colorado, Iowa, Minnesota, New Mexico, North Dakota, Oklahoma, South Dakota, Utah, Wisconsin and Wyoming.

Title in these states is usually in the form of an abstract, which is a historical summary of everything affecting ownership of the property. It includes not only the chain of ownership but also recorded easements, mortgages, wills, tax liens, judgments, pending lawsuits, marriages and anything else that affects the title. When a property is sold, the abstract is examined by an attorney, who gives a written opinion as to the title—including who the owner of record is and his judgment on whether anyone else has any right or interest in the property. The opinion is often known as the certificate of title.

Attorney's record search and opinion. In Georgia, Kentucky, Louisiana, Maine, Massachusetts, Mississippi, New Hampshire, parts of Pennsylvania, Tennessee, Vermont and West Virginia, the attorney searches the public records and issues his certificate of title.

BUYING TITLE INSURANCE

No matter what state you live in or what the customary title assurance practices are, you can arrange to purchase title insurance for a one-time charge if you wish to do so. In Iowa you can't obtain insurance within the state, but property located there can be insured by an outside company.

Title insurance companies are regulated by state law, but with the exception of Texas, rates can vary enough to make it worthwhile to shop around. All companies operating in Texas charge the same rates under state authority but compete on the services they offer.

When you're checking the fees charged by different title insurance companies, find out exactly what is covered in each case. Some routinely include the costs of handling the closing as well as the search, title report and insurance premiums. Others include just the report and premiums or, in a few states, only the premiums.

If you are getting a new mortgage, the lender will generally require mortgage (lender's) title insurance. This protects his lien on the property and makes the mortgage more marketable in the secondary mortgage market.

The face amount on the lender's policy is the amount of the loan and will decline gradually as the debt is paid off. The lender's policy does not protect you. To protect yourself, you must buy an optional owner's policy and pay an extra fee, unless you live in an area where the seller customarily provides owner's title insurance for the buyer. You can buy this kind of coverage at any time, but it is usually considerably cheaper to purchase both policies at once.

Unlike the lender's policy, the owner's policy is for the contract price and protects you and your heirs as long as you have an interest in the property. Your policy is the title insurance company's contract with you to make good any covered loss caused by a defect in the title or by any lien or encumbrance that was recorded in the public records and was not revealed to you when the policy was issued. Once you become the owner, the title company will also clear up title problems and pay for a legal defense against an attack on the title in whatever manner is provided for in its policy.

Nearly all title policies follow the same standard format, regardless of the issuing company. Take time to read it, and if possible have someone knowledge-able go over the details with you before closing. Pay close attention to what it covers and to the exceptions and exclusions. You may be offered two choices of policy, with the more expensive one insuring you against matters that affect the title to the property but do not appear in the public records.

Ordinarily, you can expect an owner's policy to cover you against such things as loss or damage from forgery, failure to comply with the law, identity of persons, acts of minors, and marital status and competency questions. Policies are sometimes amended by adding special endorsements or by removing exclusions. For example, the insurer may include a clause that will increase the face amount on the contract as your home appreciates.

One possibility for saving money and still receiving full protection is to find out whether the seller is carrying title insurance and, if so, see whether the company that holds his policy offers a reissue rate. Companies in some areas will give a buyer a cost break when they reissue insurance on a title policy made four, six or possibly even ten years ago. In many cases a reissue can also be obtained from a company other than the original issuer.

HAZARDS OF A CLOUDY TITLE

If you built a new house and failed to cover it with fire insurance and it burned to the ground, you'd still own the land. If you buy a home with a fraudulent title, you could lose everything. Title company payouts for fraud, forgery and searching errors have all increased in recent years.

There are circumstances, such as assuming an old loan or using seller financing, in which you may be tempted to save money by forgoing a title search and new owner's title insurance. The amount you save is not worth the risk. Regardless of how great a deal you've found or the customs of the region, you should obtain a title search and written opinion from an attorney or purchase owner's title insurance.

COMMON TITLE PROBLEMS

Here are examples of situations that can cloud a title. Some can be straightened out by the seller, but the buyer should have expert assistance in any event. In some, the problems may become so complicated or take so long to correct that the best solution may be to have the contract legally voided.

• You are buying a house from a single man or woman. The title search reveals two names on the ownership record and describes them as married: "John and Jane Clark, husband and wife."

• You are buying from a middle-aged brother and sister from out of town. They are selling you a home their parents bought for their retirement. The father died several years ago and the widowed mother passed away just recently. A title search reveals that the property is in her name, but there is no will on file to direct what she wanted done with it.

• You are buying from a couple who borrowed $10,000 seven years ago to add a room to their house. They have long since paid back the loan but have forgotten that her parents recorded it as a second mortgage when they made the loan. A title search shows the second mortgage but no evidence of its having been paid.

• You are buying a house to which the owner added central air-conditioning two years ago. He had a fight with the air-conditioning contractor over some damage to a ceiling that occurred during installation. When the contractor refused to correct the damage, the seller refused to pay the final installment on his contract. The contractor filed a mechanic's lien on the property.

• You are buying a house at a great bargain from a man who is in trouble with the Internal Revenue Service. IRS has placed a lien on the property.

• You are buying a property that is beautifully landscaped. A title search shows that the landscaper has a lien on the property. The seller explains that several of the trees died and when the landscaper refused to replace them, he refused to make final payment.

• You are buying a house from an aged widow. She and her husband bought the property many years ago, and when he died last year, she thought she was the sole owner. Now a title search reveals that the deed by which she and her husband acquired title was defective. The deed says only "Horace and Henrietta Jenkins." It should have shown their relationship and the manner in which they intended to take title.

• You are buying a house that has a newly paved driveway. Your seller is proud of having improved the value of his property by converting his joint driveway into a private driveway. He bought his neighbor's half in a friendly deal last year when the neighbor built a new driveway on the opposite side of his house. There is just one problem: The expanded driveway doesn't appear in the public records.

• The paving, sidewalks and gutters in front of the house you have under contract are all new. A title search shows that your seller has not paid the city's special assessment for the improvements.

• You plan to build a garage on the west end of your

lot as soon as you move in. A title search reveals an easement of 8 feet over the length of your future yard. The gas company owns the easement, which was granted by the development company that built your house.

• You are planning to get away from it all with a farmette 50 miles from town on which you are going to build a house. A title search reveals that your property was carved out of a large farm, but it was never legally subdivided. It was one of those down-home "from the apple tree on the southwest corner to the stone marker on the northwest corner" land descriptions.

That sort of inadequate land description and the resulting invalid deeds occur in the city, too, when neighbors get together and swap bits of land. Sometimes an owner with an oversized yard sells off a rear 20 feet to the abutting neighbor with a short yard. Or neighbors buy a vacant lot between them and split it. They erect a fence along the newly created lot line and consider the job finished, never thinking to get a survey and a proper deed for their new half lot and have it recorded.

Sometimes it is the owner's financial manipulations in his business that cloud his title. In the case of a bankruptcy or an unincorporated business or partnership, the owner's personal residence may be attached to satisfy part of his business debt. Another business owner may not be in trouble, just expanding, and has pledged his personal residence as part of the security required to obtain a business loan. Until that lien is paid or he arranges with his creditor to substitute other property as security, he can't deliver a clear title to you.

TO AVOID DELAYS

The examples above show why you should never, never take title to a property—not even as a gift— without full knowledge of its legal and financial condition.

Title problems, reports, abstracts and insurance policies all add to the complexity and confusion surrounding the purchase of a home. Insist on being kept informed and on understanding each step in the process. If problems come to light during a title search, remember that in many cases they can be corrected before closing.

Clearing a title can require the release of a debt or use of a quitclaim deed, for example. If the problem is only a matter of neglect, such as the failure to remove a paid-up second mortgage from the record, the task may be simple. Other cases—such as those involving contested wills—can be nightmares.

If title problems arise that may hold up settlement and you are placing a new mortgage on the property, be sure to let your lender know how much time may be necessary to clear the title. Loan commitments often expire after 30 days, sometimes earlier than that. If you don't get an extension in writing, you could lose your loan.

As soon as a preliminary title report reveals snags, confer with the title company as to whether they will be difficult to correct. If they are serious, consult an attorney on whether it is prudent to wait for their cure or to cancel your contract. Don't try canceling your contract without legal help. If it is not done exactly as the contract requires, you could be asking for a lawsuit.

HOW TO TAKE TITLE

When you buy a new home, you'll have to decide what form of ownership you want.

Married couples. The most common way for husbands and wives to own property is joint ownership, either in the form of *joint tenancy with the right of survivorship* or *tenancy by the entirety.*

Under either form if one spouse dies, the other joint owner becomes sole owner of the property. This happens automatically, bypassing probate, avoiding delays and usually trimming the costs of settling the estate. Since 1982, for federal estate tax purposes half of the value of all property owned by a married couple as joint tenants is included in the estate of the first spouse to die.

The two kinds of joint ownership differ in some respects, and many states don't recognize tenancies by the entirety. You may want to have your lawyer's advice before you take title. He will probably point out some restrictions, such as one spouse not being able to dispose of property held as tenants by the entirety without the other's consent. If you live in a community property state (Arizona, California,

Idaho, Louisiana, Nevada, New Mexico, Texas and Washington), state law will affect the form of property ownership you use.

Unmarried people buying together. There are several options to choose from.

• *Tenancy in common.* All owners have equal use of the property, but each can independently sell, mortgage or give away his interest. It's wise for the owners to have a written agreement setting out their rights to deal with their interest in the property. The agreement should also specify the percentage of ownership interest each person has in the property if, for example, they have not contributed equal amounts.

If one of the owners dies, the others do not automatically get the deceased's share unless that person specifically provides for such an arrangement in his will. If the will doesn't cover this or if he dies without a will, state law determines who gets the deceased owner's share.

• *Joint tenancy.* Under this arrangement each person has an equal interest in the property regardless of the amount contributed. If one owner dies, that person's share passes automatically to the others without going through probate.

• *A partnership.* If title is in the name of a partnership, it is the partnership that owns the property, not the individual partners. This arrangement calls for an agreement that sets forth how each partner will share in the management of the partnership.

The death of a partner does not affect the partnership; that person's heirs would acquire the interest.

This form of ownership is useful if one or more of the partners are investors who don't plan to live on the property. Another plus for a partnership arrangement is that you may avoid some problems that can arise with the other two forms discussed above if one person goes into bankruptcy or has other legal problems that could cloud the title.

American Land Title Association's

SAMPLE POLICY

BLANK TITLE INSURANCE COMPANY RESIDENTIAL TITLE INSURANCE—ONE-TO-FOUR-FAMILY RESIDENCES

OWNER'S COVERAGE STATEMENT

This Policy insures your title to the land described in Schedule A—if that land is a one-to-four family residential lot or condominium unit.

Your insurance, as described in this Coverage Statement, is effective on the Policy Date shown in Schedule A.

Your insurance is limited by the following:

- EXCLUSIONS on page _____
- EXCEPTIONS in Schedule B.
- CONDITIONS on pages _____

We insure you against actual loss resulting from:

- any title risks covered by this Policy—up to the Policy Amount

and

- any costs, attorneys' fees and expenses we have to pay under this Policy

COVERED TITLE RISKS

This Policy covers the following title risks, if they affect your title on the Policy Date.

1. Someone else owns an interest in your title.
2. A document is not properly signed, sealed, acknowledged, or delivered.
3. Forgery, fraud, duress, incompetency, incapacity or impersonation.
4. Defective recording of any document.
5. You do not have any legal right of access to and from the land.
6. There are restrictive covenants limiting your use of the land.
7. There is a lien on your title because of:
   - a mortgage or deed of trust
   - a Judgment, tax, or special assessment
   - a charge by a homeowner's or condominium association
8. There are liens on your title, arising now or later, for labor and material furnished before the Policy Date—unless you agreed to pay for the labor and material.
9. Others have rights arising out of leases, contracts, or options.
10. Someone else has an easement on your land.
11. Your title is unmarketable, which allows another person to refuse to perform a contract to purchase, to lease or to make a mortgage loan.
12. You are forced to remove your existing struc-

ture—other than a boundary wall or fence—because:

- it extends on to adjoining land or on to any easement.
- it violates a restriction shown in Schedule B
- it violates an existing zoning law

13. You cannot use the land for a single-family residence, because such a use violates a restriction shown in Schedule B or an existing zoning law.

14. Other defects, liens, or encumbrances.

COMPANY'S DUTY TO DEFEND AGAINST COURT CASES

We will defend your title in any court case that is based on a matter insured against by this Policy. We will pay the costs, attorneys' fees, and expenses we incur in that defense.

We can end this duty to defend your title by exercising any of our options listed in Item 4 of the Conditions.

This policy is not complete without Schedules A and B.

(This provision may be omitted or modified as the Company sees fit.)

BLANK TITLE INSURANCE COMPANY

By: _____

President

Attest: _____

Secretary

BLANK TITLE INSURANCE COMPANY
RESIDENTIAL TITLE INSURANCE POLICY

Schedule A

Policy Number:

Policy Date:

Policy Amount:

The Policy Amount will automatically increase by 10% of the amount shown above on each of the first five anniversaries of the Policy Date.

1. Name of insured:

2. Your interest in the land covered by this Policy is:

3. The land referred to in this Policy is described as follows:

BLANK TITLE INSURANCE COMPANY
RESIDENTIAL TITLE INSURANCE POLICY

Schedule B
EXCEPTIONS

In addition to the Exclusions, you are not insured against loss, costs, attorneys' fees, and expenses resulting from:

EXCLUSIONS

In addition to the Exceptions in Schedule B, you are not insured against loss, costs, attorneys' fees, and expenses resulting from:

1. Governmental police power, and the existence or violation of any law or government regulation. This includes building and zoning ordinances and also laws and regulations concerning:
   * land use
   * improvements on the land
   * land division
   * environmental protection

   This exclusion does not limit the zoning coverage described in Items 12 and 13 of Covered Title Risks.

2. The right to take the land by condemning it, unless a notice of taking appears in the public records on the Policy Date.

3. Title Risks:
   * that are created, allowed, or agreed to by you
   * that are known to you, but not to us, on the Policy Date—unless they appeared in the public records
   * that result in no loss to you
   * that first affect your title after the Policy Date—this does not limit the labor and material lien coverage in Item 8 of Covered Title Risks

4. Failure to pay value for your title.
5. Lack of a right:
   - to any land outside the area specifically described and referred to in Item 3 of Schedule A

   or

   - in streets, alleys, or waterways that touch your land

This exclusion does not limit the access coverage in Item 5 of Covered Title Risks.

BLANK TITLE INSURANCE COMPANY
RESIDENTIAL TITLE INSURANCE POLICY

CONDITIONS

1. DEFINITIONS
   a. *Easement*—the right of someone else to use your land for a special purpose.
   b. *Land*—the land or condominium unit described in Schedule A and any real property improvements on the land which are real property.
   c. *Mortgage*—a mortgage, deed of trust, trust deed or other security instrument.
   d. *Public Records*—title records that give constructive notice of matters affecting your title—according to the state law where your land is located.
   e. *Title*—the ownership of your interest in the land, as shown in Schedule A.

2. CONTINUATION OF COVERAGE

This Policy protects you as long as you:

- own your title

  or

- own a mortgage from anyone who buys your land

  or

- are liable for any title warranties you make

This Policy protects anyone who receives your title because of your death.

3. HOW TO MAKE A CLAIM

If anyone claims a right against your insured title, you must notify us promptly in writing.

Send the notice to _____.

Please include the Policy number shown in Schedule A, and the county and state where the land is located.

Our obligation to you could be reduced if:

- you fail to give prompt notice

  and

- your failure affects our ability to dispose of or to defend you against the claim.

4. OUR CHOICES WHEN YOU NOTIFY US OF A CLAIM

After we receive your claim notice or in any other way learn of a matter for which we are liable, we can do one or more of the following:

a. Pay the claim against your title.

b. Negotiate a settlement.

c. Prosecute or defend a court case related to the claim.

d. Pay you the amount required by this Policy.

e. Take other action which will protect you.

f. Cancel this Policy by paying the Policy Amount, then in force, and only those costs, attorneys' fees and expenses incurred up to that time which we are obligated to pay.

5. HANDLING A CLAIM OR COURT CASE

You must cooperate with us in handling any claim or court case and give us all relevant information.

Unless you can show that payment was reasonable and necessary, we will not reimburse you for money you pay, or agree to pay:

- to settle disputes

or

- to cover expenses and attorneys' fees

We will repay you for all expenses that we approve in advance.

When we prosecute or defend a court case, we have a right to choose the attorney. We can appeal any decision to the highest court. We do not have to pay your claim until your case is finally decided.

6. LIMITATION OF THE COMPANY'S LIABILITY

a. We will pay up to your actual loss or the Policy Amount in force when the claim is made—whichever is less.

b. If we remove the claim against your title within a reasonable time after receiving notice of it, we will have no further liability for it.

If you cannot use any of your land because of a claim against your title, and you rent reasonable substitute land or facilities, we will repay you for your actual rent until:

- the cause of the claim is removed

or

- we settle your claim

c. The Policy Amount will be reduced by all payments made under this Policy—except for costs, attorneys' fees and expenses.

d. The Policy Amount will be reduced by any amount we pay to our insured holder of any mortgage shown in this Policy or a later mortgage given by you.

e. If you do anything to affect any right of recovery you may have, we can subtract from our liability the amount by which you reduced the value of that right.

7. TRANSFER OF YOUR RIGHTS

When we settle a claim, we have all the rights you had against any person or property related to the claim. You must transfer these rights to us when we ask, and you must not do anything to affect these rights. You must let us use your name in enforcing these rights.

We will not be liable to you if we do not pursue these rights or if we do not recover any amount that might be recoverable.

With the money we recover from enforcing these rights, we will pay whatever part of your loss we have not paid. We have a right to keep what is left.

8. OUR LIABILITY IS LIMITED TO THIS POLICY
This Policy, plus any endorsements, is the entire contract between you and the Company. Any title claim you make against us must be made under this Policy and is subject to its terms.

12

Taking the Shocks Out of Settlement

This is the last hurdle

Y ou are only days away from getting a house in your name. You defined your ideal and went determinedly searching for it. You turned the market upside down to find a good mortgage. To stay in your price range, you had to make some compromises on the house and on the financing. You had the property inspected from gutter to garret and found some things you didn't like but decided to tolerate.

The search has been expensive in terms of both time and money. Now it's time for you to pay for the property and for the seller to deliver the deed.

There is no standard term for this next step. Depending on where you live, it is known as title closing, settlement or closing of escrow.

The closing officer in your area may be a title company, an abstract company, an abstract attorney or a regular real estate attorney. Occasionally it is a broker or a lender. *Never deal with an owner without a legally responsible third party involved to handle the closing.* Every deal needs such a party to make sure all the contract's requirements are lived up to before any money is disbursed or the title is passed.

When closing involves an actual meeting, the process is commonly called settlement. If no meeting occurs, it's often known as escrow and is handled by an escrow agent. In escrow cases, the buyer and seller typically sign an agreement requiring each party to deposit certain funds and documents with the agent. When all the papers and monies are in, the escrow is "closed." The agent records the documents and makes the appropriate disbursements.

Settling on a home ought to be as serene as a treaty signing. Too often it's as full of static as a debate in the United Nations. Peaceful closings are planned closings. Each party knows what to expect.

THE COSTS YOU FACE

One key to a shockproof settlement is to get estimates of your charges as soon as possible. You probably had ballpark figures to work with when you first started looking, but once your purchase offer was accepted, you should have received more detailed estimates from the agent and from the various lenders with whom you made application.

Your overall settlement costs are influenced by, among other things, where you live, your settlement date, how you finance your purchase and what the particular lender requires to provide the loan. The federal government's Real Estate Settlement Procedures Act covers most of today's home loans, including VA, FHA, FmHA or other government-backed or -assisted loans; loans from lenders with federally insured deposits; loans eligible to be purchased by GNMA, FNMA or in other federally related secondary mortgage markets; and loans made by lenders who invest or make more than $1 million in residential loans each year. Assumptions and seller financing are not covered by RESPA.

If you've applied for a new loan from a lender who is covered under RESPA, the law requires that you be given a "good faith" estimate of fees when you make a written loan application—or soon after—and that you be offered a pamphlet titled *Settlement Costs and You* put out by the Department of Housing and Urban Development. This contains a description of how the closing process works and explains terms you will encounter in your transaction.

The day before settlement you are entitled to see the Uniform Settlement Statement. This is a copy of what you will get at settlement. (In places where there is no meeting, the escrow agent may arrange for you to get a copy when escrow is closed.)

Use the worksheet in this chapter to check the lender's and agent's estimates against actual amounts as you get them. This may provide you with some advance warning if there are substantial changes before settlement. The worksheet, like HUD's Uniform Settlement Statement, breaks the total settlement charges into six broad categories:

- Costs associated with getting a loan.
- Items the lender will get you to prepay at closing (mortgage insurance, for example, or hazard insurance).
- reserves for insurance, taxes and assessments.
- title assurance costs.
- recording and transfer charges.
- additional fees for attorney services, etc.

You may want to run through the worksheet and note which items are to be paid in full or in part by you. Local custom usually influences whether the buyer or the seller pays a particular charge. You can do things differently, but to avoid conflicts, make sure your purchase contract states clearly how each item is to be handled. Otherwise, it's not unreasonable for the seller to expect you to abide by the prevailing custom.

In some areas, for example, the buyer pays for a title insurance policy because the buyer's lender requires the protection. In other places the seller absorbs that charge as one of the selling costs. In some areas the buyer always pays the local recordation tax; in others the seller always pays it. In some jurisdictions they split it. Points on conventional loans are often apportioned between buyer and seller. Ordinarily, lenders are prohibited from charging points on FHA and VA loans, but they may charge an origination fee.

In most cases, payments made to obtain financing will make up the largest proportion of your settlement costs. Take this hypothetical case to see what closing costs might be involved for a purchaser of a $100,000 home. The contract calls for a $20,000 down payment. The buyer gets a 30-year, $80,000 FHA mortgage at 12%. Settlement is January 2.

Credit report	$ 50.00
Loan origination fee*	800.00
Interest from January 2 to February 1 @ $26.67 per day for 30 days†	800.10
Property tax reserves‡	160.00
Hazard insurance reserves§	57.50
Title insurance policy (lender's portion)**	220.00
New hazard insurance policy	345.00
Closing fees	96.00
Recording fees	15.00
Total	$2,543.60

*Loan origination fees are charged by the lender and are commonly 1% of the loan amount. On an FHA mortgage the buyer ordinarily cannot be required to pay more than 1%, or one point. In a conventional sale, however, he could pay more. Depending on the cost of money at the time of the purchase, your points could be the largest expense at settlement.

†Because the buyer's first regular monthly payment won't be due until March 1, the lender collects the first month's interest at closing.

‡Lenders frequently collect part of the annual property tax at settlement and hold them in reserve until due. In such cases buyers are required to pay 1/12 of their property tax each month with the mortgage payment. How much is paid at settlement depends on the closing date and how taxes are assessed and collected in the area.

§The lender sets aside funds collected at closing to help pay hazard insurance premiums. Flood and mortgage insurance premiums are also often collected in advance.

**See Chapter 11 for a discussion of title insurance.

The buyer's closing costs may include such additional charges as an appraisal fee, the owner's portion of title insurance, assumption fees (if the buyer is taking over the seller's mortgage), mortgage insurance and points. The total settlement costs are ordinarily less if the buyer is assuming a loan or paying cash rather than getting a new loan.

BE PREPARED TO NEGOTIATE

If closing practices call for a face-to-face meeting and you feel you are basically getting a good deal, you may wish to compromise in order to resolve disputes that arise. Say some unexpected expense shows up— one you might reasonably be expected to absorb but are completely in the dark about. A squabble at this point, especially one that puts you in a legally questionable position or one that pits you against local custom, may delay closing, create additional costs and lead to lawsuits. At this point it's often best to compromise.

SETTLEMENT OR ESCROW COSTS WORKSHEET

	Agent's estimate	Lender's estimate	Actual
Costs related to obtaining a loan			
Loan origination fee	_____	_____	_____
Loan discount, or points	_____	_____	_____
Appraisal fee	_____	_____	_____
Credit report	_____	_____	_____
Inspection fee	_____	_____	_____
Mortgage insurance application	_____	_____	_____
Assumption fee			
_____	_____	_____	_____
_____	_____	_____	_____
Items to be paid in advance			
Interest from _____ to _____ @ $_____ per day	_____	_____	_____
Mortgage insurance for _____ to _____			
Hazard insurance for _____ years to _____	_____	_____	_____
_____			
Items to be deposited with lender at settlement			
Hazard insurance _____ months @ $_____ per month	_____	_____	_____
Mortgage insurance _____ months @ $_____ per month	_____	_____	_____
City property taxes _____	_____	_____	_____
County property taxes _____	_____	_____	_____
Annual assessments _____	_____	_____	_____

Title costs
Settlement or escrow fee ___ ___ ___
Abstract or title search ___ ___ ___
Title examination or opinion ___ ___ ___
Title insurance binder ___ ___ ___
Document preparation ___ ___ ___
Notary fees ___ ___ ___
Attorney's fees (including the
   charges listed above)

_____ ___ ___ ___

Title insurance (including the
   charges listed above)

_____ ___ ___ ___
Lender's coverage ___ ___ ___
Owner's coverage ___ ___ ___

_____ ___ ___ ___

_____ ___ ___ ___

Recording and transfer charges ___ ___ ___
Recording fees:
   Deed $_____
   Mortgage $_____
   Releases $_____ ___ ___ ___
City/county:
   Deed $___ Mortgage $___ ___ ___ ___
State:
   Deed $___ Mortgage $___ ___ ___ ___

Other costs
Attorney's fee ___ ___ ___
Buyer/broker fee ___ ___ ___
Pest inspection ___ ___ ___

_____ ___ ___ ___

_____ ___ ___ ___

TOTAL SETTLEMENT OR
  ESCROW CHARGES ___ ___ ___

13

Tax Angles of Home-ownership

You get a break from Uncle Sam

It's a long haul from poring over the newspaper ads on the kitchen table to signing on the dotted line at the settlement table. If you suffer from trepidation or frustration along the way, you can fight it off with the knowledge that making what may be the biggest investment of your life also means buying into what's probably the best tax shelter you'll ever enjoy.

The concept of homeownership as the American dream is fully endorsed by the nation's tax laws, which have turned homeowners into a privileged class of taxpayers. Under orders from Congress, Uncle Sam stands ready to serve as a generous partner in your investment.

How generous? Exactly how well you will fare depends mostly on your tax bracket. But overall, it is estimated that in 1982 the federal government indirectly reimbursed homeowners for more than $28 billion worth of their monthly payments. You got it:

$28,000,000,000. That's how much Americans saved on their federal income tax bills by deducting the mortgage interest and property taxes paid on their homes. The value of other federal tax breaks—such as the gentle way the law treats the profit you stand to make as your house appreciates in value—isn't included in that $28 billion figure; neither are the state tax benefits you earn when you buy a home.

Though the tax breaks attached to homeownership are no secret, they aren't all as well understood and easy to take advantage of as the interest and tax deductions. Just as buying a house promises to cut your tax bill, it guarantees to complicate your tax life. If you don't already do so, you're almost sure to have to begin itemizing deductions. Even if you've itemized before, the purchase or sale of a home will involve you in an especially complex tax return. Although you don't need to be able to cite chapter and verse of the tax law and regulations, you need a general awareness of the rules if you are to take advantage of them.

This review of the tax benefits of homeownership is designed as a refresher for the veteran homeowner as well as a primer for the first-time buyer.

THE TAX SIDE OF BUYING

A key attraction of any house is the built-in tax breaks. The opportunity to trade nondeductible rent payments for mostly deductible mortgage payments was probably high on the list of reasons that got you into the housing market in the first place. When squeezing your budget to determine how much house you can afford, you know you have to consider both the actual monthly outlay and the after-tax cost of various offerings.

In the early years of a traditional mortgage, nearly all of each monthly payment is deductible interest. That's disappointing from the standpoint that it means you are paying off only tiny bits of the loan principal. But it's great in terms of tax savings.

On a $100,000, 30-year traditional mortgage at 13%, for example, the interest and principal payments would total $13,274 annually. In the first year, nearly $13,000 of that amount—almost 98% of it—would be deductible interest. Even in the 15th year of the mortgage, almost 87% of the payments would serve as tax-saving write-offs on the home buyer's tax return. Not until the 26th year, in fact, would he reach the point at which more than half of the payments went to principal. All of what you pay for local property taxes each year is deductible, too, whether you have a mortgage or not.

How much those deductions are worth to you depends on your marginal tax bracket. That's the percentage of each dollar that would have to be turned over to the Internal Revenue Service if you weren't spending it on a deductible expense. The following table lists the tax brackets for 1983 for married and single taxpayers. The "taxable income" figures represent gross income—salary, business income, dividends, capital gains, etc.—minus all adjustments, excess itemized deductions and exemptions.

| Joint returns | | Single returns | |
taxable income	tax bracket	taxable income	tax bracket
$16,001–$20,200	19%	$12,901–$15,000	21%
20,201– 24,600	23	15,001– 18,200	24
24,601– 29,900	26	18,201– 23,500	28
29,901– 35,200	30	23,501– 28,800	32
35,201– 45,800	35	28,801– 34,100	36
45,801– 60,000	40	34,101– 41,500	40
60,001– 85,600	44	41,501– 55,300	45
85,601–109,400	48	over 55,300	50
over 109,400	50		

Say you file a joint tax return and your taxable income for the year is $55,000. You are in the 40% marginal tax bracket. For each $1,000 that mortgage interest and real estate tax deductions reduce your income within that bracket, your tax bill would be cut by $400. Remember that these same deductions can also trim your state income tax bill. For home buyers in the top tax brackets, more than half of their interest and tax outlays is returned via state and federal tax savings.

Adjust withholding. You don't have to wait until you file your tax return to see the benefit of all your tax-saving deductible expenses. As soon as you purchase your first home or buy a new place that involves higher deductible expenses than your previous house, you probably can direct your employer to begin withholding less tax from your paychecks.

To reduce withholding, you should file a revised W-4 form with your employer. You can get a copy of the form, and the instructions for it, from the personnel office where you work or from your local IRS office. Follow the instructions to see how many extra withholding allowances you may qualify for as a result of your new deductions. By curbing the government's withholding bite, you can boost your take-home pay just when the extra cash will come in especially handy.

What's your basis? The basis of your home is its value for tax purposes, your total investment in the place. It is the figure you compare with the amount you get for the place when you sell to determine whether you have a taxable profit. Although it begins simply enough as what you agree to pay for your home, the basis will change often between the day you buy and the day you sell. And, as discussed later, the basis of each home you own can affect the tax basis of the next one you buy. You have to keep track of all adjustments to your basis to ensure that you're not overtaxed.

This record-keeping chore begins with sorting out the tax consequences of the closing costs you pay at settlement. Although a few of these expenses may be deducted in the year of the purchase, most are considered part of the cost of acquiring the house and are added to the basis.

First, consider the deductible closing expenses, since they have the most immediate financial consequences:

• *Points you pay to get your mortgage*. These are deductible as interest in the year paid provided they are an additional charge for the use of the borrowed funds, rather than points to cover loan-processing fees or other expenses associated with the loan.

Assume, for example, that to get a 15%, $40,000 mortgage, you have to pay the lender three points ($1,200). You can write off the $1,200 on the tax return for the year of the purchase, in addition to the interest paid as part of your monthly payments. Points charged in connection with a VA mortgage, however, are not deductible. Because the government sets the maximum interest rate that can be charged on VA mortgages, points in addition to that rate are considered payment for services rather than additional interest.

• *Prepaid interest or property tax adjustments.* If your closing costs include reimbursing the seller for interest or real estate taxes he has paid in advance— for a period during which you actually own the home—you may deduct those amounts as though you had paid the interest or taxes directly. Even if such adjustments don't show up on the settlement sheet, you can deduct them. If you don't directly reimburse the seller, the prepaid amounts are considered to be included in the price of the house. In that case, you should reduce your basis by the amount you deduct for prepaid interest and taxes.

Additional closing costs and other acquistion expenses probably aren't deductible unless you qualify to write them off as job-related moving expenses, which are discussed later. Instead, many of these costs are added to the purchase price and raise your basis. Since additions to basis usually don't produce any immediate tax savings, you might be tempted to ignore them. But that could be a costly mistake.

Sooner or later, you are going to have to know the adjusted basis of your house, including those settlement costs. The higher your basis when you sell the place, the lower the amount of potentially taxable profit you have to report to the IRS. Maintaining detailed records from the beginning is not only the best way to assure accuracy, it's also a lot easier than trying to reconstruct your basis later on. Set up a file now to keep a running tab of your adjusted basis.

Besides the purchase price, the following acquisition costs can be included in the basis of your home:

• State and county transfer taxes.
• Appraisal and credit report fees.
• Mortgage origination and assumption fees.
• Attorney and notary fees.
• Recording and title examination fees.
• Property inspection fees.
• Title insurance premiums.
• Utility connection charges.
• Amounts owed by the seller that you agree to pay, such as part of the selling commission or back taxes and interest.
• The cost of an option if you purchase under a rent-with-option-to-buy deal. It is also possible that part of the rent payments made prior to closing may be added to the basis if they were applied to the purchase price. Check with a tax attorney or accountant about how payments under your contract should be treated.

THE TAX SIDE OF OWNING

It's easy to take advantage of the basic tax benefits—the deductions for mortgage interest and property taxes. If your mortgage is held by a financial
institution, you will receive a statement early each
year showing how much deductible interest you
shelled out in the previous year. The statement will
also show the amount you can deduct for property
taxes if you make those payments through your
lender. Otherwise, your copies of the tax bills and
your canceled checks provide the information you
need to work on your tax return.

Your tax situation can be more complicated if your
mortgage is held by an individual or you are buying
with the help of more exotic creative financing. The
specifics of your arrangement will determine what
part of your payments is deductible and what portion
isn't.

Assume, for example, that the seller holds a
$10,000 second mortgage that calls for interest-only
payments for three years and a balloon payoff of the
entire principal at the end of that period. In this case,
all of your payments on the note during the three
years would be deductible as interest. Unfortunately,
though, not all arrangements are so straightforward.

Consider the zero percent interest plans, described
in Chapter 4. The buyer gets to deduct part of the
payments on such a deal even though the stated
interest rate is 0%. As far as the IRS is concerned, for
tax purposes these loans are treated as though they
carry built-in interest at a rate of 10%, compounded
semiannually.

How much the buyer can deduct on a 0% mortgage depends on the repayment schedule. No part of the payments made during the first six months after the sale is considered interest, but after that a portion of each payment is deductible. On a five-year loan with equal monthly payments, for example, more than 20% of each payment (after the first six) is considered interest; on a seven-year 0% deal, almost 30% of the payments can be deducted as interest.

Buying with a 0% mortgage also affects the basis of the home because the sales price is considered to include all of the interest that can be deducted over the life of the loan. The original basis of the home would be the stated price minus the unstated interest. Consider this example: A house is sold for $90,000 with $30,000 down and the $60,000 balance payable in monthly installments over five years. The unstated interest on this deal would total $12,370, so the cost basis would be $77,630—the $90,000 price minus the $12,370 of unstated interest.

Though the IRS decided in 1982 how taxpayers should handle 0% mortgages, it hasn't cleared up all the tax questions about some other sorts of creative financing. As of early 1983, for example, the IRS was still trying to sort out all the tax angles involved in shared-appreciation mortgages.

You should have a clear understanding of the tax consequences of your deal before you sign a contract. If an individual is providing financing, you may need to sit down with a tax attorney or accountant to discuss any complicated twists involved in your purchase.

Local assessments. In addition to real estate taxes, it is not unusual for local governments to assess homeowners charges for services or benefits provided during the year. Such fees are becoming more and more common in some areas as local officials search for ways to increase revenues while trying to hold down property taxes. These bills should go into your tax file because, depending on what a charge is for, it could be either a deductible expense or an addition to your basis.

• In general, assessments for benefits that tend to increase the value of your property—for a new sewer, for example, or new sidewalks—should be added to the basis of your property.
• Special charges for repairs or maintenance of local benefits, such as sewers or roads, however, can be deducted as additional local taxes.
• Fees assessed for specific services, such as trash or garbage collection, are not deductible, nor can they be added to your basis.

Improvements and repairs. Any homeowner will tell you that monthly mortgage payments are just the beginning of the costs of owning a home. You can count on spending plenty of time and money over the years maintaining, repairing and improving your property. And here, too, Uncle Sam gets involved.

Work around the house has to be divided between projects that are considered repairs and those that constitute capital improvements. It's an important difference. Repairs are considered nondeductible personal expenses, but the cost of improvements, though also nondeductible, can be added to the basis of your property.

To qualify as a capital improvement, the expense has to add value to your home, prolong its life or adapt it to new uses. Adding a bathroom, paving a driveway and putting in new plumbing or wiring are examples of improvements that increase your basis.

Repairs, on the other hand, merely maintain the home's condition. Fixing a gutter, painting a room or replacing a window pane, for example, would be considered repairs rather than capital improvements. In some cases, however, the cost of projects that would ordinarily be considered repairs—such as painting a room—can be added to the basis if the work is done as part of an extensive remodeling or restoration of your home. Also, some major repairs—such as extensive patching of a roof—may qualify as improvements.

There is no list of what the IRS considers improvements. They're often judgment calls, and two IRS agents could disagree over a specific expenditure. But the better your records, the better your chances of pushing up your basis to reflect improvements on your property. Keep detailed records of any work done that *might* qualify as an improvement. It's better to keep records that might not be needed than to toss out a receipt that could save you money. In addition to saving receipts and canceled checks, you may want to make notes to remind yourself exactly what was done, when and by whom.

When totaling up the cost of improvements, include the cost of materials and labor. Although you can count what you pay hired workers, you are not allowed to add anything for your own time and effort if you do the work yourself. You should, however, include any incidental costs involved. If you pay to have your lot surveyed as part of installing a fence around your property, for example, the cost of the survey can be added to your basis.

Energy credits. When you spend money for certain government-sanctioned improvements, you can earn a tax credit as well as boost your basis. The Congress has created two federal tax-credit programs to encourage energy conservation. A tax deduction permits you to reduce your taxable income, but a credit is more valuable because it can be used to offset your actual tax bill dollar for dollar.

The first program promises a tax credit worth 15% of up to $2,000 you spend for approved energy-saving items installed in your principal residence. The $300 cap (15% of $2,000) applies to your house; it's not an annual limit. Although you don't have to use up your entire credit in one year, the total amount claimed for any one home can't exceed $300. If you move to a new principal residence, you renew your $300 credit level.

Another restriction on the credit is that it is available only if the approved items are installed in a principal residence built before April 20, 1977. If your home was not substantially completed by that date, you can't qualify for this credit.

If you qualify, you may claim the credit for 15% of the cost of installing the following items in your home:

- Insulation.
- Storm or thermal windows or doors.
- Caulking and weather stripping for doors and windows.
- Automatic setback thermostats.
- Furnace replacement burners, flue opening modifications, and ignition systems that replace gas pilot lights.
- Meters that show the cost of energy use.

When figuring the addition to your basis for these items, count the total cost, including what you pay for installation, minus the amount of the tax credit you claim.

The second program offers a bigger tax credit for homeowners who install renewable-energy equipment to provide power for their principal residences. Uncle Sam will foot the bill, via a tax credit, for 40% of the cost of qualifying solar, wind or geothermal energy equipment. The 40% credit can be applied to as much as $10,000 worth of improvements, meaning it can knock as much as $4,000 off your tax bill. If the credit amounts to more than your tax bill for the year, you can apply any unused portion to what you owe the following year. You can qualify for this credit regardless of when your home was built.

Many states offer similar tax breaks to encourage the development of alternative energy sources. If you consider a project of this type, be sure to check whether it qualifies for the tax benefits.

THE TAX SIDE OF SELLING

You don't have to file any forms with the IRS when you buy your home or when you make basis-boosting improvements. But when you sell, the government wants to know the details. After all, there might be a tax to be collected . . . although there is a good chance the transaction won't add a dime to your tax bill.

When you sell your home, you will realize how clever you've been to follow advice on keeping records offered earlier in this chapter. To determine the tax consequences of the sale, you have to know the adjusted basis of your home, a value you should be able to compute easily based on the information in your files.

Your profit or loss is the difference between your adjusted basis and the amount you realize on the sale. The amount realized is the selling price minus the costs connected with the sale, such as commissions, advertising and legal fees. (In some cases, these selling expenses can be deducted as moving expenses, an advantageous alternative that is discussed later.)

If your bottom line shows a loss, it is not deductible. However, if you prepaid your mortgage in connection with the sale and incurred a prepayment penalty, you can write off that amount as interest paid.

In the more likely event that your home sale produces a profit, your capital gain may be taxable in the year of the sale, in a later year or never, depending on your circumstances. The chance to put off or completely avoid tax on the profit is one of the most valuable tax benefits for homeowners.

Deferring the tax bill. If you have already purchased or plan to buy another home, you may be able to postpone paying tax on your profit. To qualify, you must buy and occupy another principal residence within a specified replacement period, which encompasses the two years before and the two years after the sale of your house. If you are in the armed forces or living abroad, you may qualify for an even longer replacement period that would give you up to four years after the sale to buy and occupy a replacement home.

Basically, if the house you buy costs at least as much as the one you sold, you get a reprieve on paying tax on the profit from the sale. The profit is considered to be reinvested, or rolled over, into the new home.

Assume, for example, that you realized a $30,000 profit when you sold your old home this year for $100,000 and that you buy another home for $125,000. Rather than pay tax on the $30,000 profit, you reduce the basis of the new home by that amount. Its adjusted basis thus becomes $95,000. If you later sold that home for $135,000 ($10,000 more than you paid), you would show a profit of $40,000—the $30,000 rolled over from the first house plus the $10,000 appreciation of the second. You could postpone the tax bill again by buying a replacement home for $135,000 or more.

If you choose a replacement home that costs less

than the one you sell, you'll owe tax on the amount by which the *adjusted sales price* of the old home exceeds the cost of the new one. The adjusted sales price is usually the same as the amount realized on the sale, but it can be less if prior to the sale you incurred qualifying fix-up expenses, such as the cost of painting and repairs to make the home more attractive to buyers. These expenses come into play for tax purposes only if your replacement residence costs less than the one you sold. In such cases, the expenses—which must be for work done during the 90 days before you signed a contract to sell and paid for within 30 days afterward—are subtracted from the amount realized to determine the adjusted sales price. That, in turn, can boost the amount of profit on which tax is deferred.

Assume, for example, that you sell for $100,000 a home with an adjusted basis of $70,000, and that you buy a replacement home for $90,000. Of the $30,000 profit on the sale, $20,000 would be rolled over into the new home, giving it a $70,000 basis. The other $10,000 would be taxable in the year of the sale.

If you had incurred $1,000 worth of fix-up expenses, however, you could defer the tax on $21,000, so that only $9,000 of the gain would be taxable: The basis of the new home would drop by $1,000, to $69,000, to reflect the extra $1,000 deferred profit.

What if you plan to buy a replacement home but haven't closed the deal by the time your tax return is due? You may still postpone the gain. You would simply fill out the first part of the tax form used to report the sale of a home (Form 2119) and note that you intend to buy a new home during the replacement period. If the house you buy costs enough that you can defer the entire gain, all you have to do is notify the IRS of that fact and file a completed Form 2119.

If you don't buy in time to take advantage of the deferral, or if the house you buy costs less than the one you sold, you have to file an amended tax return (Form 1040X) for the year of the home sale. On that form, you would report the amount of profit to be taxed. The IRS would charge you interest on the tax bill from the time the return was due until you paid the bill.

There is no limit on the number of times you can use the deferral technique to put off tax on the profit that builds up while you own a house. The fact that profits can be rolled over from one home to the next means the basis of your first home can affect the basis of your last—a point that reemphasizes the importance of detailed record keeping.

There is a restriction, however, that generally prevents you from doing this more often than once every two years. Assume, for example, that you sold one house in January 1983 and deferred tax on the gain by buying another home the same month. Then in August 1983 you sold that home and bought another one. The rules prohibit postponing tax on the gain from the sale of the intermediate house. However, because in this example the third home was purchased within two years of the time the first one was sold, the profit from the first house is considered to be reinvested in the third. You would have to pay tax only on the profit that accrued during the months you owned the second house. But even this restriction is waived if the home sale is connected with a job-related move that qualifies you to deduct moving expenses.

If you don't buy a replacement residence, all of the profit from the sale of your home would be taxable unless you qualify for the exclusion discussed below. If you owned the home for a year or less before the sale, the profit would be taxed as ordinary income. More than a year of ownership, however, means you treat the profit as a long-term capital gain, so only 40% of it would be taxed.

The $125,000 exclusion. This is the icing on the cake for homeowners, a major exception to the rule that profit from the sale of a home is taxed unless you buy a new, more expensive home.

If you are at least 55 years old when you sell your home, you may be able to escape the tax completely on up to $125,000 of profit on the deal. To qualify for this tax break, you also must have owned and lived in the house for at least three of the five years leading up to the sale. If you are married and the house is jointly owned, you can qualify as long as either you or your spouse meets the age, ownership and residency tests.

This tax break is a once-in-a-lifetime opportunity, and the exclusion can be applied to only one home sale. You can't use part of the exclusion to shelter $50,000 profit on one home, for example, and later use the rest of the exclusion to avoid tax on the sale of another home. If you use any part of the exclusion, you use it all.

Married couples are limited to a single $125,000

exclusion, and if one spouse used the exclusion before marriage, that scotches the other spouse's right to it as long as they are married.

Although available only once, the exclusion can serve to exempt from tax the profit on several houses, thanks to the deferral of gain from one home to another. When you decide to use the exclusion, the profit that has built up in any number of homes over the years—up to $125,000 worth—can be sheltered.

Seller financing. You report the sale of your home on Form 2119 ("Sale or Exchange of Principal Residence") and attach it to your tax return for the year of the sale. That form will show how much profit you made on the sale, whether any of it was rolled over into a new home, whether any of it was excluded under the 55-and-over tax break and whether any of it is taxable. If part of your profit is taxable, you have to report that amount on Schedule D ("Capital Gains and Losses"), too.

If you helped finance the sale, your tax picture gets more complicated. In addition to reporting the sale on Form 2119, you have to deal with the tax consequences of the payments you receive from the buyer.

If you are either deferring the tax on your profit or using the exclusion to shelter it, payments you receive on the note may be a combination of return of your basis (which would be nontaxable), a return of your gain (either deferred or excluded) and interest on the loan (taxable as ordinary income). You should report the interest income on Schedule B along with any other interest you earned during the year.

The exact tax treatment of the payments would

depend on your specific arrangement. If you are receiving interest-only payments on a note that calls for a balloon payment of the principal at a later date, for example, all of that interest is taxable as you receive it. If your deal involves a 0% mortgage, you have to report as interest income the same amount of unstated interest that the buyer gets to deduct each year.

If part or all of the gain on the sale is taxable, and you will receive at least part of the payment from the buyer after the close of the year of the sale, you may report the profit on the installment basis: Rather than have a big bulge in your taxable income for a single year—which could push you into a much higher tax bracket—you could report and pay tax on the profit as you receive it in the future. Another potential money saver, if you have to report any or all of the profit, is to use the income-averaging method to figure your tax bill for the year.

Owning a home can be a great tax shelter, and selling one can call for some tax planning. Even if you normally prepare your own tax return, it could be well worth your while to consult a tax attorney or accountant before filing for a year that involves a home sale. Just as you worked hard to get the best possible price for your home, you should invest some effort to get the best possible tax deal.

MOVING EXPENSES COUNT, TOO

Buying a new house is often part of a move to take a new job. If your purchase is connected with a job switch, you may rack up more tax benefits. Many of the expenses involved in the move, including some of the costs of selling your old place and buying the new house, may be deductible on your tax return.

To qualify to claim these deductions, your new job must be at least 35 miles farther from your old home than your old job was. If you former job was 10 miles away from your old home, for example, your new job must be at least 45 miles away from that old home. Note that it doesn't matter how far your new home is away from your new job site.

In addition to the 35-mile test, to be eligible to deduct moving expenses you must work full time for at least 39 weeks during the 12 months after the move (and at least 78 weeks out of the first 24 months if you are self-employed).

If you qualify, here's what you can deduct:

• The cost of trips to the area of the new job to look for a new house. There's no requirement that the house-hunting expedition be successful for the cost to be deductible.
• The cost of having your furniture and other household goods shipped, including the cost of packing, insurance and up to 30 days' storage.
• The cost of getting yourself and your family to the new hometown. Include the cost of food and lodging on the trip.
• The cost of food and lodging for up to 30 days in the new hometown if these temporary living expenses are necessary because you have not yet found a new home or it is not ready when you arrive.

• Certain costs associated with the sale of your old house and the purchase of the new one. These expenses—including real estate commissions, legal fees, state transfer taxes, appraisals and title fees— are the same costs discussed earlier as potential additions to the basis of the house you buy or reductions in the amount realized on the place you sold. If you qualify to write off moving expenses, you can choose whether to deduct these costs in the year of the move or use them as adjustments to your basis. It's usually beneficial to count them as deductible moving expenses.

There is a dollar limit on the amount you can deduct for buying and selling expenses, however. Your write-offs of those expenses, plus those for house-hunting trips and temporary living expenses, can't exceed $3,000. And of that total no more than $1,500 can be for house-hunting expeditions and temporary living expenses. There is no dollar limit on how much you can deduct for the cost of shipping household goods or travel expenses. Any reasonable amount you paid can be deducted on your tax return.

If your employer reimbursed you for your moving expenses, the amount will probably show up on your W-2 form for the year. Whether or not it does, you should report the reimbursement as income, which you will offset by claiming your moving expense deductions.

PART TWO

FOR SELLERS

14

Before You Hang That "For Sale" Sign

Ask yourself: Is this sale necessary?

Do you need to sell or are you just thinking about it? If selling is anything less than a necessity, consider the points in this chapter before you call in an agent. Once you involve real estate professionals, you may be swept toward a decision you are not ready to make or one that may not be in your best interest.

It's a rare agent who will come in and advise you not to sell, but in the real estate environment of the '80s, staying put may be the smartest decison. If you must sell, move on to the next chapter. Otherwise, give some thought to reasons for staying put.

KEEPING YOUR GAIN

Say you had the good sense or good fortune to become an owner before the booming inflation in home prices of the 1970s and the huge hike in interest rates that followed. Selling means giving up those advantages.

Times have changed. No longer can you count on rising home prices to give you a big profit every few years. If you bought your present home at a price that would be a steal today, you would give up all that gain if you plow everything into a bigger home at a more inflated price.

REMODELING COULD BE A BETTER WAY TO GO

Many homeowners feeling pinched for room or eager for a more modern home have looked at the housing market and decided to remodel. They prefer to take on a shorter-term remodeling debt rather than buy an entire house at current prices and rates. So extensive has this trend become that in 1982 expenditures for remodeling nearly matched the $50 billion spent on new homes.

Before you decide to buy a different house or take on a new mortgage, find out what it would cost to refurbish your home with the features you want. If you took out a loan for remodeling, your monthly housing cost could still be less than what you'd pay for a new mortgage. Even if the combined payments were equal or higher, your payback period on the remodeling loan could be shorter than that for a new mortgage, and the total interest cost could be less.

PROFITS ARE ONLY PART OF IT

It's axiomatic in financial planning that you don't liquidate an investment until you have a place to reinvest the money.

Getting in and out of the home market is a lot more cumbersome—and more expensive—than getting in and out of the stock or bond market, especially when you have a household full of goods and a family to consider.

There are tax consequences, too. In most cases if you sell your home and don't reinvest the profit in another home within two years, the profit is taxable as capital gain. (See Chapter 13 for information about the special $125,000 exclusion for taxpayers 55 years or older.)

If you are selling to realize a profit and don't plan to buy another home, then you are confronted not only with the inevitable tax and reinvestment questions but also with the cost of replacing your living space. Often owners who consider their homes pure investments fail to calculate the cost of disrupting their households and providing alternative living space as part of the cost of the alternative investment.

Homeowners who decide to become renters often find the transition a difficult one. Among the problems: Rental space that affords the amenities of a well-appointed home can be very expensive and, in some areas, hard to find at any price.

MAYBE YOU NEED AN EQUITY LOAN

The age-old frustraton of being equity-rich and cash-poor can lead you to consider selling if you have substantial medical, college or other bills to pay. Before you commit yourself, find out what banks, savings and loans and other lenders are offering in the way of equity loans. These loans came into vogue a number of years ago when lenders realized that many homeowners had a rich source of untapped equity because of the steep increase in the market value of their homes.

The market value of your home relative to the balance of the mortgage loan determines the amount of equity you have and what you can borrow. A typical lender's formula subtracts the amount owed from the appraised value (one determined by a lender-approved appraiser) and then multiplies the remainder by 80%. For example, if you owe $50,000 on your mortgage and your home is appraised for $90,000, you may be able to borrow up to $32,000.

THE COST ADVANTAGE OF STAYING PUT

While the cost of housing was rising as fast as or faster than inflation and the cost of money remained relatively cheap, you could easily trade up and the only consequence was a somewhat higher monthly payment. Many homeowners sold one home and bought another to get a new kitchen, central air-conditioning or even a new start on decorating, since they had big profits tied up in the house but no cash to make major improvements.

If you plan to sell your present home in order to buy a more expensive one that suits your needs better, you should consider not only the price spread between your old home and your new one but also how much extra you will be paying for such things as mortgage interest, real estate taxes, insurance and utilities.

Say your original loan was $60,000 at 10% for 30 years, making the monthly payment $526 for principal and interest. Change the rate to 13% for the same amount over the same period and your payment becomes $663.

But that doesn't begin to tell the whole story. If you are trading up, the chances are you will be taking on a bigger debt. If you are buying a $100,000 house and using the $25,000 you got out of your old house as the down payment, you would need a loan of $75,000. At 13% on $75,000 for 30 years, your monthly principal and interest payment is $790. At 14% your payment becomes $889.

Assume the balance on your current 10% mortgage is $50,000 (down from the original $60,000). With any fixed-rate loan, most of the payment in the early years goes to interest. If you have paid off $10,000, that means your loan is approximately 15 years old and that just over 20% of your payments are going toward paying off the principal balance.

If you sell and take out a new loan, you are right back at the beginning of an amortization schedule. That means a bigger tax deduction but only a tiny accumulation of equity. With a 30-year, $75,000 loan at 14%, only about $15 (or roughly 2%) of your monthly payment of $889 goes toward equity in the first year. You also have to consider the cost of points you might have to pay for the new loan as well as other up-front expenses involved in buying a home.

Those comparisons are based on fixed-rate mort-

gages. If your new loan is an adjustable-rate one
without a ceiling on either interest rate or payment,
you will have to make comparisons based on the
initial period or on assumptions about future interest
rates. (See Chapter 4 in Part 1 for a discussion of
adjustable-rate mortgages.)

No matter how you do it, real estate transactions
cost money. If you sell through an agent, you will pay
6% or 7% or whatever percentage of the selling price
is being charged as commission fees by brokers in
your area. When you buy, the commission and settlement costs may be passed along to you in the price of
the house. One way or another, you will be paying a
substantial percentage of the price of the property in
service fees. Obviously, it is a lot cheaper to stay put.

15

Polishing Up The Merchandise

Once you've decided to sell

If you want top dollar for your home, give yourself every break.

There's nothing you can do to help your sale so much as dedicating yourself to a thorough spit-and-polish campaign before you put it on the market, even before you call the first broker. If you are selling it yourself, you have to be equally or perhaps even more meticulous.

The broker is usually the first person you have to sell. The attractiveness of your home is his clue as to how easy or how hard a "peddle" it may be. Its appearance may even influence his opinion of value because he knows that homes that show well bring better prices than those that don't. A run-down, shabby, dirty or cluttered home is not likely to get a big bite of the firm's advertising budget, nor is it going to be staffed with the better agents at an open house. Used homes are like used cars: The shiny, well-kept ones sell first, and no one is so keenly aware of that as the brokers and agents who spend their lives going in and out of other people's homes.

One of the things that makes living in a "for sale" house hard—and it is hard—is that you have to live in a showroom. That doesn't mean you have to be on display all the time, but it does mean that you'll have to keep up on even minor repair jobs and maintain a more rigid than normal standard of housekeeeping.

GET YOUR PLACE IN SHAPE

Now is the time to do all the touchups and maintenance needed to get the property to pass muster with an eagle-eyed buyer or a professional inspector looking it over for an interested buyer. You may have put up for years with a torn screen in the basement window, a loose tile in the bathroom or paint scratched off the front door by the dog, but if you fail to remedy such things before you put your home up for sale, you risk creating an atmosphere of neglect.

Using the list at the end of this chapter as a guide, pretend you are a building contractor and walk through your home working up a list of everything that needs to be done. Make notes as you go along. When you've completed your inspection, go back and jot down what you can do to make each room look attractive. If could be taking down dark drapes, removing fingerprints from a door frame and waxing the floor, or it might involve repapering a wall or replacing a marred bathroom sink.

Unfortunately, you can never anticipate where a

prospective buyer will focus his attention when he enters your home. A buyer might breeze past plaster walls and a new furnace but stand scowling at a cracked toilet tank top. Or he may spend hours evaluating the heating and plumbing systems but never notice the fresh paint, refinished floors and brand-new windows.

SALES TRICKS THAT WORK

Make your home look as spacious as possible. You accomplish that by getting rid of everything extraneous, admitting as much daylight as possible and keeping the place shipshape. Now, not later, is the time to have your big sorting out party. Inventory what you are going to sell, give away or throw away when you move. Then take action. Crammed closets, messy garages or carports, overfurnished rooms, spilling-over bookcases, triple-stacked china cupboards, attics and basements with a flea-market look—all clutter turns buyers off. Many of them don't mention it, but agents can see the chill coming over them. Some find it distasteful, others find it oppressive, as though they had to cope with all that. Whatever the reaction, it is always negative.

Depersonalize your home. Tuck away the distractions. That includes the bedroom wall full of family pictures.

Why put away the clan pictures? Because such an open display of rootedness and family can distract one kind of client who becomes fascinated with it and wants to know all about it. That's a minus—he's distracted. You want to sell him your home, not your family. Another kind of client is embarrassed by it. It makes him feel he is intruding, a not uncommon problem in showing an occupied home. And you are always risking a third sort: the fellow who is reminded of someone he can't stand by the picture of your Uncle George.

What you are trying to do, after all, is to help the client visualize himself in your home. If it is so indelibly stamped with you that he can't identify with it as his future home, you've chased away a customer.

Neutralize it. An even more important kind of distraction to get out of sight is all clues to your sentiments regarding political and social causes. No matter what your views are about the President, your senators and congressman, Jane Fonda, gun control, abortion, ERA, the Mideast, welfare or anything nuclear, keep it to yourself. Get out of sight all your banners, bumper stickers and partisan literature, including magazines. Which would you rather do, make a statement or sell your house? More often than the layman suspects, you can do one or the other but not both. Customers don't talk about what displeases them, they just walk away.

MAKE SURE EVERYONE KNOWS WHAT'S FOR SALE

If you list your property for sale with a broker, read the listing agreement carefully and tell your broker any problems or defects in the property you are aware of. If you are acting as your own broker, tell your potential buyers. Failing to do so can cause you to lose a sale or become entangled in a lawsuit. If the listing agreement doesn't adequately spell out the current condition of the structure, the appliances and the electrical, mechanical and plumbing systems, you may want to do so in a letter.

In most cases it is the language in your sales contract that will determine what has to be in working order at settlement. Many contracts provide that the mechanical equipment is in working order. If any of it is not, you should write in the exceptions. The laws and customs where you live may become the deciding factor if your contract is not clear. Say that only three of the four burners on your stove work, and you don't want to pay for repairs. If your contract doesn't show that the sale included the stove "as is"—with three burners, not four—you may be faced with having to pay for the repairs at settlement.

For some things, such as a window air-conditioner that doesn't work, you may find a buyer interested in negotiating the matter. Regardless of the situation, your best protection (and the buyer's) is a detailed and carefully drawn sales contract and pre-closing inspection by the buyer. Getting the buyer's signature on a statement that he has inspected—and accepted—the property just before closing is an important protection for you.

TAKE A FRESH LOOK AT YOUR OLD HAUNTS

Use this inspection guide to see your home as a buyer might.

INSIDE

Attic

Check underside of roof for leaks, stains or dampness.

Look around chimney for condensation or signs of water.

Clean and clear ventilation openings if necessary.

Walls and ceilings

Check condition of paint and wallpaper.

Repair cracks, holes or damage to plaster or wallboard.

Windows and doors

Check for smooth operation.

Replace broken or cracked panes.

Repair glazing.

Check condition of weather stripping and caulking.

Examine condition of paint.

Test doorbell, chimes, burglar alarms.

Wash windows if necessary.

Floors

Inspect for creaking boards, loose or missing tiles, worn areas.

Check baseboards and moldings.

Test staircases for loose handrails, posts, treads.

Bathrooms

Check tile joints, grouting and caulking.
Remove mildew.
Repair dripping faucets and shower heads.
Check condition of painted or papered walls.
Test operation of toilet.

Kitchen

Wash all appliances.
Clean ventilator or exhaust fan.
Remove accumulation of grease or dust from tiles, walls, floors.

Fireplace

Inspect dampers, firebox, hearth, screen and mantel.
Check condition of paint and mortar.

Basement

Remove clutter.
Check for signs of dampness, cracked walls or damaged floors.
Inspect structural beams.
Check pipes for leaks.

Electrical system

Check exposed wiring and outlets for signs of wear or damage.
Repair broken switches and outlets.
Label each circuit or fuse.

Plumbing system

Look for leaks at faucets and sink traps.
Clear slow-running or clogged drains.
Bleed air off radiators if needed and check for leaking valves.

Heating and cooling systems

Change or clean furnace and air-conditioning filters.
Have equipment serviced if needed.
Clean area around heating and cooling equipment.

OUTSIDE

Roof and gutters

Repair or replace loose, damaged or blistered shingles.
Clean gutters and downspout strainers.
Check gutters for leaks and proper alignment.
Inspect flashings around roof stacks, vents, skylights and chimneys.
Clear obstructions from vents, louvers and chimneys.
Check fascias and soffits for decay and peeling paint.
Inspect chimney for loose or missing mortar.

Exterior walls

Renail loose siding and check for warping or decay.
Paint siding if necessry.
Check masonry walls for cracks or other damage.
Replace loose or missing caulking.

Driveway

Repair concrete or blacktop if necessary.

Garage

Lubricate garage door hinges and hardware.
Inspect doors and windows for peeling paint.
Check condition of glazing around windows.
Test electrical outlets.

Foundation

Check walls, steps, retaining walls, walks and patios
for cracks, heaving or crumbling.

Yard

Mow lawn, reseed if necessary.
Trim hedges, prune trees and shrubs.
Weed and mulch flowerbeds.

16

Setting the Right Price

Not too high, not too low

Being able to set the right price on a home is one of the most important skills in real estate. And it's never so important as when there are more sellers than buyers.

You will be better off if you determine the correct price and then stick to it, rather than set an arbitrarily high figure and let bargaining "find" the right price.

Careless overpricing can cost you time, and worse than that, it can tarnish your real estate. Once your property gets the reputation for being overpriced, both the experienced real estate agents and the savvy buyers will shun it. The more serious a buyer gets, the tighter the circle of properties and agents in which he moves. A knowledgeable buyer close to making his choice may have found out as much as any single broker about what's being offered and how long it has been on the market.

The first thing both the buyer and the broker want to know about a seller is whether he is serious about selling or on a fishing expedition. "Fishing expedition" is real estate slang for the posture of holding to an unrealistically high price in hopes of catching a buyer—the fish—who doesn't know any better.

Fishing expeditions work in wild sellers' markets when buyers are competing to buy. This is what occurred in Southern California in the late 1970s, when there were so many more buyers than there were houses for sale. Some sellers offered their property at auction, starting with very stiff minimums, and still the buyers lined up for hours in advance to get a chance to bid. It was all part of the frenzy of buying a house as an inflation hedge and buyers didn't seem to care how much they paid as long as they could pay for it with "creative financing."

Inexperienced sellers imagine it is a good idea to start a little high because you can always come down. Sometimes the attitude is, "Let's start high and see how it goes; I'm in no hurry." This is poor strategy. *All that overpricing usually accomplishes is to attract idle shoppers and would-be buyers without money while driving serious buyers away.*

Real estate brokers prefer to spend advertising dollars only on well-priced properties. Your broker won't promote your home intensively if it is overpriced (even if he did agree with you on the price in order to get your listing).

If you are selling the place yourself, the high cost of classified advertising will eat into your profit fast if you stubbornly cling to an unrealistic price. Even if you hook a fish, chances are you won't be able to reel in a naive buyer if he needs a loan to finance the purchase. The appraiser for the lender will be guided by the market, not your price, in setting a loan limit for the property.

Underpricing is a danger, too, but a rare one. You run the risk of underpricing, just as you do overpricing, if you pick a number that sounds right to you without having something solid to base it on. Unless you are in a frightful hurry, there is no reason for not trying to get full market value. Occasionally, owners will deliberately price property low to move it in a hurry, motivated perhaps by grief after a death, anger after a divorce or a desperate need to raise cash fast. Underpriced properties rarely hit the listing books. When they do, they don't stay there long because the professionals snatch them up.

HOW TO GET PRICE INFORMATION

Research comparable homes—that's the only way to find the right price. You have to know all about the sales of property like yours. Be realistic about the market you are operating in. If you are in a bear market, you'd better not have a bull price. To be comparable for appraisal purposes, the house has to be nearly identical to yours in age, style, size, condition and location. You cannot compare your home with a house on the other side of town, no matter how similar it may be in construction and layout. Start your research by learning about the recent sales in your immediate neighborhood. Try to find comparable sales no more than six months old, and get at least three of them.

It is just as important to know the terms under which a house was sold as it is to know its price. A $100,000, all-cash sale is very different from a $100,000 sale with $10,000 down and a $20,000 second trust carried back by the seller. Sales between friends or relatives are usually not suitable for comparisons, either.

You also need to know the condition of the property. If the house was recently decorated or carpeted or if the owners added expensive features, such as an extra bath, those are essential elements in comparing that home with yours when it comes to matching prices. Your county assessor may be helpful in providing information on which to base adjustments in comparing properties.

The timing of the other sales is critical, too. Typically, prices are softer in a down market, so if you are offering yours in a better market, you should be able to add something to your price.

Shop your competition. Whether you are using a broker or not, it's useful to know what houses similar to yours are being offered for. Keep in mind, though, that *asking* prices are not always *taking* prices. One way to gauge how well your neighbors priced their property is to find out how long it was on the market.

You can get information on sales you are interested in at the courthouse or city real estate tax office. In jurisdictions where there is a tax on the transfer of property, you can determine the price by the tax paid. For example, if the tax or fee is 0.1% (.001) of the sales price and the transfer document is $77, then the price paid by the buyer was $77 divided by .001, or $77,000. Property records are open to the public, but the information may be hard to decipher or of limited usefulness.

You won't learn anything at the tax office about the terms of the sale, the style of the house, its state of repair or how long it was on the market. Your best bet for getting that kind of information is to copy the names and contact the buyers and sellers themselves.

Don't rely on the assessed value of your house as a reliable guide to its market value. Assessments are likely to be far under the market price or out of date. It's good to be aware of that fact, though, because a buyer may try to use the assessed valuation as a bargaining weapon to beat your price down.

AN OBJECTIVE APPROACH

Intelligent pricing combines objective evaluations of both the property itself and the market conditions at the time of the offering. No matter how good the condition of your home, if it is in an area where values are falling because of the loss of a major employer or heavy competition from a neighborhood of unsold new homes close by, your price will be adversely affected. Conversely, if your home is in an area that has become a popular place to live, it will likely bring as good a price as your neighbor's even if it is not quite so bright and shining.

The most scientific way to go about pricing your home is to hire a residential real estate appraiser. (See Chapter 9 for a discussion of what to ask for and the names of national professional organizations.) An appraisal not only helps you set the price sensibly but also gives you a valuable tool for evaluating brokers interested in working for you. The more you know about your property, the better position you are in to test their straightforwardness and familiarity with the market in your neighborhood. Be on guard against flattering free appraisals given by brokers more interested in getting a listing than in giving you good advice.

What you pay for an appraisal can be added to your other selling expenses for tax purposes. The appraisal may also help you hold to your price, especially if you plan to do your own selling. Let the buyer know you have an appraisal that may be acceptable to the lender he is using; that could save him the cost of another report.

The asking price you ultimately set may be higher than the value placed on the property in the appraisal, but in most cases it shouldn't be substantially higher. If you are in a position to offer below-market financing, or if you have an assumable loan, inform your appraiser so that he can take that into consideration. Some appraisers will give you two prices if you ask—one that cashes you out, with the buyer making a down payment and getting a new loan for the difference, and a higher price for a deal that includes seller financing.

If your house is in the moderate price range, you might want to consider a VA or FHA appraisal. Thanks to a change in policy, you now need only one appraisal to sell to either a VA or an FHA buyer. If you get a VA appraisal and then find a buyer who obtains an FHA loan, the FHA will accept your existing appraisal. Getting this kind of appraisal doesn't mean you have to sell VA or FHA. You may want to use it only as a pricing guide and selling tool.

The cost for a VA or FHA appraisal varies with the locality. A typical charge for a single-family home is about $85. A condominium appraisal costs more, usually about $130. With this kind of appraisal you get a certificate of reasonable value from the VA and a conditional commitment on the FHA, rather than the more detailed kind of report you'd expect from a residential appraiser.

FHA limits the size of the mortgage it will insure to $67,500 to $90,000, depending on where the property is located. (In Hawaii and Alaska borrowing limits go up to $135,000.) The maximum VA loan guarantee is $27,500, but the loan amount can exceed $100,000. Total borrowing limits vary among lenders but are frequently calculated as four times the guaranteed amount. Ceilings on both programs are adjusted periodically.

THE PRICE IF YOU'RE THE LENDER

If you are going to offer seller financing, try to raise the price of your home enough to compensate for not being able to invest some of that loan at market rates and for the higher risks that may be involved. Perhaps you can find out what price premiums were set on homes comparable to yours that sold over the past few months. In recent years homes sold with the aid of seller financing commonly commanded 10% to 15% premiums.

How much you can add to the price of your home depends on a number of factors, including: How quickly do you need to sell? What kind of financing can you offer and at what interest rates and terms? What are the current market conditions?

What's important to you as the seller is how much you will net out of the deal. If you are going to hold paper—a second mortgage, for example—you need to determine what it would be worth if you were to turn around and sell it immediately. If you would have to accept a substantial discount, you are in effect taking a cut in price.

17

Do You Want to Be the Lender?

Watch out for potential pitfalls

Before you put your property on the market, decide whether you want to become a lender and, if so, what kinds of financing you are going to offer. Discuss possible plans with a competent real estate attorney and your broker to assess whether they meet your needs. Then price your property accordingly and have the loan written and processed in a manner that makes it both insurable and salable.

You can avoid most pitfalls by having your seller financing prepared by a professional lender and by insuring the mortgage with private mortgage insurance.

PLUSES AND MINUSES

Being a lender usually involves substantial sums of money and is always a serious investment decision. To be in a position to be a primary lender, you have to have either a debt-free home or one with a small balance on the existing mortgage. First mortgages are commonly for 70% to 80% of the purchase price.

Among the concerns you as a primary lender should have is that if you use the buyer's down payment to pay the balance on your existing loan, you could come out of settlement with little or no cash. On the plus side, if the loan is properly drawn, executed and recorded, it would likely put you in a strong position in the event of default because in most states a purchase money mortgage takes priority over other mortgages, liens and judgments recorded against the property.

Second mortgages often spell the difference between a sale and a collapsed negotiation. They commonly bridge the gap between the price of the property and the combined amounts of the down payment and first mortgage. In many cases the buyer will assume the existing first mortgage at the same rate or a new, blended rate. Seconds are usually short-term and traditionally carry a higher interest rate than first mortgages. This reflects the greater degree of risk involved. Second mortgages typically account for 10% to 30% of the purchase price, and this often means the seller is leaving his profit in paper. A second mortgage is written much like a first but usually makes reference to the first and takes a junior position to it in the event of default. If a foreclosure sale brings only enough money to cover the first mortgage, you as the holder of a second mortgage could lose your total investment.

A large proportion of seller financing involves

short-term balloon notes. Sellers receive monthly payments based on a fixed interest rate and as if the loan amount were amortized over 20 or 30 years. But at the end of a specified period, say three or five years, the remaining balance is due in one lump sum.

When these arrangements became popular, buyers and sellers were operating under the assumption that when the balloon came due, interest rates would be lower, properties would be worth more and refinancing would be relatively simple. In thousands of cases, those assumptions proved to be excessively optimistic. If you plan to offer your buyer financing that includes a balloon payment, consider carefully the consequences to you if when the balloon came due, you were faced with having to extend the deadline to avoid foreclosing.

You would also be wise to have your attorney insert a clause that bars assumption of your loan. Some of the sorriest experiences in seller financing resulted when the buyer sold the property (along with the seller's loan on it) to irresponsible people. Typically, such a buyer-turned-seller gets enough money from the sale to get his own cash out, leaving the original seller to worry with a new buyer. If the new buyer is a poor credit risk or has purchased a property that is too expensive relative to his income, you could have a long-term problem on your hands. He may be unable to refinance the balloon; he may be slow to pay; you may have to foreclose.

If you don't want to automatically bar an assumption, your attorney may suggest a clause that will give you the right to review the credit of and approve any buyer who wishes to assume the loan.

RUNNING A CREDIT CHECK

Whatever you do, don't decide the buyers are "nice" people, ask a question or two about their employment and let it go at that. Though professional lenders take the position that they are lending primarily on the value of the property and secondarily on the creditworthiness of the applicant, they still take every precaution to prevent the expense and hassle of foreclosure. So should you.

The sales contract should provide for the charges made by a professional lender to run a credit check on the buyer and to prepare the loan. You may also want to arrange for the loan to be serviced at the same time. If you are acting as your own broker, the contract should be contingent on your receiving from the buyer a complete credit history and satisfactory report from a recognized credit investigative agency. Make sure you know the following:

- Name, age and address of the buyer or buyers.
- Number of dependents and their ages.
- Amount of the preferred down payment.
- Maximum down payment possible.
- Source of down payment.
- Amount of the preferred monthly payment.
- Maximum monthly payment the buyer could carry.

• Employment information for each wage earner: name and address of employer, position, length of time in that position, length of employment with previous employers.
• Average monthly income.
• Total earnings before taxes for the last three years.
• Outside income.

It is important, too, to get a picture of the buyer's net worth. For that you have to get a complete list of his assets and his liabilities. This will tell you how much in debt your buyer already is (how many installment loans he carries, how much merchandise he has bought on credit, whether there are any judgments against him, whether he owes alimony or child support payments) and give you an idea of his general financial situation and whether he has any assets to fall back on in the case of temporary unemployment.

Professional mortgage lenders use several rules of thumb to judge whether a buyer can handle a particular sale. Though they might relax one of the following criteria if the buyer is strong on the others, they would be reluctant to advance credit to someone who is weak in more than one area. How does your potential buyer stack up?

• His total housing expense (principal, interest, insurance, taxes) would not be more than 28% to 33% of his stable monthly income (the income that is likely to continue in the future).
• All of the buyer's monthly debts that are expected to continue longer than ten months should not exceed 38% of his stable monthly income.

• The buyer should invest at least 10% of his own cash in the purchase.

• The buyer's credit history should be good, and in particular he should have no record of any delinquency or default against a previous mortgage loan.

MAKE SURE THE LOAN CAN BE INSURED

One major risk of sellers who finance the sale is loss from default. Another is getting stuck with a purchaser who is always behind in his payments or can't find refinancing for the balloon when it comes due. Despite these pitfalls, sellers often agree to real estate arrangements involving thousands of dollars with less caution than they would exercise if they were making a $1,000 cash loan. Problems frequently stem from failing to adequately check the creditworthiness of the borrower, lending too much in proportion to the price and making balloon loans with unrealistically short terms.

If you are taking back a first mortgage, you will generally need less insurance coverage than if you are taking a second, since you would need to cover only the costs of foreclosure and carrying the home until you could sell it again. On a second mortgage you may need to insure up to 80% or more.

A number of companies offer insurance for seller financing plans, including the Mortgage Guaranty Insurance Corp., PMI Private Mortgage Insurance and Ticor Mortgage Insurance. These companies usually operate through approved commercial lenders, who charge for preparing and managing the plan. The origination fee is normally paid by the buyer at closing and may be 1% to 2% of the loan amount. The buyer also usually pays the insurance premiums. The seller pays for the cost of servicing the insurance—perhaps ½ of 1% to 1% of the annual loan payments.

The lender who prepares the loan will evaluate the creditworthiness of your buyer, prepare the loan documents and other necessary papers. The lender may also service the loan, i.e., collect and process the borrower's payments, provide monthly escrow services to assure you that taxes are collected and hazard insurance kept in force, and give you and the buyer regular accounting statements. Your agreement will also probably call for the lender to manage late payments and default proceedings.

Though not every plan insures every type of seller loan, you should be able to get coverage for a first mortgage, a second mortgage, a deed of trust, a contract for deed or a wraparound. To be eligible, your property and the loan papers will have to meet the insurer's requirements. If you want default coverage on a balloon payment note, for example, you may be required to offer to renew or refinance at the market rate when the balloon comes due. Find out the specific requirements for the plans available to you before you get into negotiations with prospective buyers.

COULD YOU SELL YOUR PAPER?

It used to be that if you helped your buyer by giving him a loan, you were obliged to hold the paper yourself unless you were willing to sell it to an investor, usually at tremendous sacrifice. Investors wouldn't buy them unless they could get them for 30 to 50 cents on the dollar.

Sellers now have direct access to a national secondary market—the Federal National Mortgage Association—for their paper. Fannie Mae, the nation's largest single purchaser of home mortgages, will buy qualifying new and existing seller first or second mortgages. The maximum loan amount for a single-family home is $108,300. (There are higher limits for two-to four-family dwellings and for homes in Alaska and Hawaii.)

If Fannie Mae owns the first mortgage on the property, the combined amounts of the unpaid principal on the first and second mortgages cannot exceed $108,300. If Fannie Mae doesn't own the first, the limit applies only to the second mortgage. For owner-occupied properties the unpaid balance on a first mortgage may be up to 95% of the value of the property. The combined balances on a first and second can be up to 80%. Thus, if a house is worth $98,000 and has a $50,000 first-mortgage balance, Fannie Mae will not buy a second mortgage of more than $28,400.

The top 25% of the second mortgage must carry private mortgage insurance if the first and second balances exceed 65% of the home's value. In the example above, if the buyer makes a $30,000 down payment, assumes the $50,000 first and receives an $18,000 second mortgage from the seller, Fannie Mae will require insurance on $4,500 of the second.

Fixed-rate and adjustable-rate mortgages are eligible. Fully amortizing second mortgages may run 3 to 15 years, and balloon seconds may have terms of 5 years.

First mortgages exceeding an 80% loan-to-value ratio must carry private mortgage insurance.

If you plan to sell your loan to Fannie Mae, the mortgage must be serviced by an approved lender. The fee is negotiable and varies from lender to lender. Plan on passing the cost on to the borrower, since he is the one who benefits.

If you sell your loan, it will be discounted to yield Fannie Mae's prevailing market rate. The term and type of loan also affect what Fannie Mae will pay. If you take back a 15-year balloon (30-year amortization) second mortgage for $25,000 at 13% and Fannie Mae's required yield at that time is 15%, for example, you will receive $22,096 (less the lender's fees). To find out the current discount, call an FNMA-approved lender (a broker can give you names of ones in your area, or call the nearest regional office of Fannie Mae).

Keep in mind that other buyers of seller loans may have underwriting criteria that differ from Fannie Mae's. Their names and requirements should be available through real estate brokers and mortgage bankers.

18

Searching for a Broker

Who is right for you?

If you want to turn the work of selling your home over to a broker who will relieve you of most of the strain, be prepared to invest some time and energy in the search. Choosing the right broker may not make selling your home a cakewalk, but it can make the difference between a well-orchestrated campaign and a frustrating ordeal. This is, after all, the person you are going to trust, depend on and take advice from regarding one of your principal assets. You don't have to like him in the sense that you hope to make him a lasting friend, but you'd better be able to communicate with him. No matter how successful the broker is, if his personality and selling style set your teeth on edge, you'll be better off with someone else.

Whoever you select should have a reputation for integrity and a proven track record selling homes in your area. A broker who has been running a successful business for several years has developed contacts and resources in a community. You should be able to find out how he and his firm are regarded by lenders, lawyers and former clients.

CHECK OUT THE FIRM

Once you've narrowed the competition, use the following guidelines to help you make a final selection.

Find out how intensely the firm works your area. The thing to be impressed with is not how many listings a firm carries but the percentage of its listings that it regularly sells. Don't be taken in by a flurry of action. A firm that goes in for heavy advertising or a blitz of "For Sale" signs may be so eager to gain a foothold in an area that it is taking listings from semiserious sellers at any price.

Check out the company's reputation and experience. Don't pick a brokerage firm just because you like an individual agent. When you give a listing, you are picking a company, its track record for service and its relationship with other brokers. As a practical matter, most of your contact may be with the agent, but you need to be sure there is strong supervision, administrative backup and plenty of technical expertise behind that agent. To whom will your agent turn for advice if problems arise? The heavy-duty financial work, contract preparation and counseling are usually provided by the broker.

Is the firm staffed mostly by full-time agents? How many are part-timers? How experienced are the agents as a group? Do they concentrate on selling homes or are they also involved in commercial real estate and property management?

How does the firm handle client calls? One way to find out is to call as though you were a prospective buyer for one of its listings. Naturally, when you call in as a seller, you're almost sure to get a royal welcome, no matter who answers the phone. The agent taking your call becomes the listing agent and so stands to get a cut of the commission even if someone else eventually sells it. If, on the other hand, you are calling as a purchaser about a house listed by another agent, the welcome you get may be less enthusiastic.

What you want to find out, of course, is what your potential buyers are likely to hear. In many instances you will be asked for your phone number so that the listing agent can call you back. Keep track of how long it takes to have your call returned. If the listing agent is away from the office, pay attention to how carefully the message is taken. Does the agent answering the phone have enough information at hand, or are you kept hanging while he searches for a file or someone who is able to talk to you? Do you get alert and enthusiastic responses? Does the agent seem interested in telling you about the property you called about, or does he try to switch you to something else?

There are great differences in styles of brokering. Some agents are high-profile, hard-sell people who work the numbers—if the first tries don't move the property, they put it on the back burner and go on to a different one. Others are low-profile, soft-sell types who work with the client, solve the problems, bulldog it through. If yours is an easy home to sell, the fast and furious way may be for you. If it's going to take some patient problem solving, either because of your selling conditions or because you're in a buyers' market, you will probably do better with the steady, persistent approach.

INTERVIEW YOUR FORMER NEIGHBORS

If you want to learn how well a broker has performed, look up sellers who have used his firm. Don't go to your new neighbors—they were the buyers. Seller satisfaction is what you are interested in.

There is no reassurance as valuable to you as the testimony of a pleased seller. From conversations like these you can learn things that are just not obtainable any other way.

Don't stop with one seller. You may have to jog your memory to recall the houses in your area that have sold over the past six months or year, but the hours spent on this investigation should save weeks, even months, of aggravation that comes from being tied up with the wrong broker.

When interviewing your former neighbors who have sold, have a list of questions and a method for organizing the answers so that you come out of each interview with comparable information.

Before you get to specific questions, ask them for an overall rating of their broker. It's as important to know whom to avoid as whom to employ.

Here's a list of questions for a seller.

- How long was the house on the market?
- Did it sell for the original price or did you have to make adjustments?
- With how many brokers did you have your home listed? If more than one, what happened to the other one(s)?
- Did the broker withdraw voluntarily, or did you refuse to renew the listing? Either way, why?
- Do you think your broker got you the best deal in both price and terms that was available at the time, or did you take the deal because you had to make a decision without more delay?
- Did the entire office push your house, or did the job fall pretty much to the listing agent?
- Do you think your broker and his firm made it easy or hard for other firms to cooperate?
- Did the firm maintain a strong selling push, or did you have to keep prodding them?
- Do you think the property could have been sold faster by someone else? For more money?
- Did the broker see you through the closing?
- Were the people you dealt with courteous?
- Did they call for appointments to show your home and call to cancel when they had a change of plans?
- Knowing what you know now, if you had to do it all over again, would you use the same broker?

The broker who is already active in your area may have interested clients for your house even before he runs the first ad. Knowing the appraisal history of an area, what each property sold for and the terms under which it sold is a powerful selling tool. If a client says he thinks your price is high, there is no better rebuttal than for an agent or broker to tick off the facts about every recent sale in the area, particularly when he can say, "We made those sales."

Sometimes, knowing the circumstances behind a sale is especially important, and for that a broker almost has to have been party to it. If a client who has done his homework argues that your house is priced $7,000 higher than the similar house that was sold across the street, your agent should have an answer. Making a guess like "Maybe it wasn't in such good shape" won't be good enough. It will be much better if he can say, "We sold that house during the worst of the recent housing depression, when interest rates were so high that nine out of ten people who looked at it couldn't qualify for the loan. The seller was in no position to carry any of the financing, so he elected to take a price cut instead. The person who bought it paid all cash."

WHAT KIND OF LISTING?

Once you've selected one or two brokers you'd be comfortable working with, you are ready to talk about listing your property. A listing, whether oral or written, exclusive or nonexclusive, is an employment contract. One of the earliest decisions you have to make is whether you want one full-time broker or several part-time brokers.

Getting the most intensive sales promotion for your property doesn't necessarily mean employing the most brokers to work in competition with each other.

In fact, what often happens is that if no broker is protected, no broker takes any responsibility. A broker won't spend money advertising a property, thus exposing it to other brokers, unless he is guaranteed some part of the sales commission. He has that guarantee only if he is the exclusive listing broker, as explained below.

If you sign a listing agreement, don't let yourself be tempted by a client who breaks away from the broker and tries either to throw the sale to an agent friend in a competitive company or to go behind the broker and buy from you directly to shave the commission from the price. If you sell directly to a client produced by a broker, you are asking for a suit over the commission. You must be meticulous about the source of the client if you want to stay out of a fight.

If your property is so competitively priced, is in such excellent condition and is so well located as to produce this kind of interest, you may want to consider selling it yourself. (See Chapter 19, "Being Your Own Middleman.")

Here are your choices of listing arrangements.

Exclusive right to sell. This is the most common type of listing. The listing broker is entitled to a commission no matter who sells the property—even if it's you. He can share that commission with another broker under a cooperative arrangement, in which case they divide the commission between them. You are guaranteed that you will be charged only *one* commission.

An exclusive right to sell generally assures you the most service. In return for your contractual protection of exclusivity, the broker pledges to you his best effort in procuring a contract that is advantageous to you. It's a simple trade-off: The broker is assured of a commission if he produces a sale, and you have someone you can hold responsible for making that sale.

Exclusive. This arrangement is the same as the one above except that you retain the right to sell the property without paying the broker a commission. As a practical matter you won't find many brokers willing to take this form of listing unless you have a specific client who became interested in your house through your efforts before the broker came on the scene but you aren't sure whether that deal will really go through.

Nonexclusive, or open. This listing is used if there is no multiple listing service. The listing may be extended to one or several brokers simultaneously. It provides that a commission will be paid to the broker who procures the sale, yet it allows the owner to find a buyer without owing a commission. With this listing the broker is under no obligation to promote your property in any way.

Oral agreements. Most states require that listings be written. In some places oral listings are still valid, and you may be just as obligated to pay a commission with an oral listing as with a written one if the broker produces a deal.

With any kind of listing, if the broker brings you the deal that the listing calls for (full price, exact terms offered by a buyer who is ready, willing and able to

*buy), you are obligated to pay him a commission
whether you accept the sale or not.*

THE LISTING AGREEMENT

The listing agreement should cover a definite period of time and show when and how it may be renewed or terminated. It will show the price and the amount of commission. Commissions are negotiable, and some brokers work for less than others, but in most cases you can expect to pay between 6% and 7% of the actual selling price.

If you expect the property to sell very quickly or there are special circumstances to consider, let the agent know you would like to negotiate the commission or make other changes in the agreement. If you pay less than is customary, be sure the listing agreement is clear about what will be done for you in the way of advertising and promotion. What are you expected to do that would otherwise be done by the firm? Keep in mind that if the cut is too deep, cooperating brokers may not be interested in working for a percentage of a small commission.

The commission is usually deducted from the proceeds of the sale at closing but may be paid in some other way. In any case, this should be spelled out in the listing agreement and in the sales contract.

A listing should also cover the personal property included or excluded from the sale and contain information about schools, churches, recreation and shopping in the area.

You should get a copy of the agreement. As the days go by, your agent should keep you informed about what he is doing to promote the property, send you copies of ads, and keep you up-to-date on the response they bring. After showing the property, he should let you know how prospective buyers reacted.

If you are not satisfied with your agent's performance, you may mutually agree to cancel the listing at any time. However, terminating the contract without cause can lead to a bill for services or perhaps legal complications.

Before you sign an exclusive listing, your agent should do several things.

• Go through your home with you, pointing out repairs and other things you can do to make it more appealing. He may measure the rooms or arrange to have that done later.

• Give you information about the housing market in general and the current activity in your neighborhood. Ask him how long similar properties listed with him have taken to sell in recent months.

• Prepare a market analysis and research all recent transactions in your area to help you decide on an asking price.

• Discuss what you can expect in the way of advertising and promotion. Will the house be held open on weekends? How will it be shown and during what hours? If your agent is a member of a multiple listing service, your listing will be circulated through the system. This means any cooperating agent may become a subagent if he finds a buyer for the property.

If you don't want that much public exposure, you can request that the listing be kept out of MLS, but you must make your request in writing.

• Prepare a data sheet showing how much you can expect to realize on the sale, using different financing arrangements. If you are considering offering seller financing, he should have the knowledge and experience to guide you. He should be familiar with the sources of funds—private and institutional—in the community.

• Explain the listing agreement and answer all your questions.

19

Being Your Own Middleman

"For Sale by Owner"

Maybe you would like to try your hand at playing broker and save that 6% or 7% sales commission. Any sale requires the services of a middleman, whether you perform the chores or pay someone else to do them.

In 1978 and 1979, when it seemed as if every other person had real estate fever, all many owners had to do to sell their homes was be there to open the door. The rest was routine paperwork. Buyers weren't shopping for property, they were grabbing it.

The '80s are a tougher market. The number of able buyers is far fewer. There is a great deal of frustrated demand among would-be buyers for whom affordability is the critical issue.

Financing is always important to real estate; in the '80s it is more crucial than ever. If you are willing and able to grapple with the financing problems (see Chapters 16 and 17), you are halfway to making a sale. It is important not to underestimate the time or work involved, though. Just putting your home on display won't be nearly enough.

GOING IT ALONE

If you decide you want to handle the sale yourself, these are the resources you will need:

• Plenty of time to show your home during daytime hours, as well as at night and on weekends.
• Patience with the public. This one is easy to underestimate unless you have experience with other kinds of selling, handling complaints or doing volunteer work.
• A talent for selling. Do you have a nose for sniffing out the real buyer as distinguished from the window-shopper? Does the prospect of displaying the merchandise, fielding the buyer's questions, overcoming his objections, helping him solve his problems and then winning appeal to you? If not, or if it impresses you as indelicate or undignified, you had better call a broker.
• A willingness to get the facts you'll need about both pricing and financing, or to pay someone else to get them.
• A good real estate lawyer. Not just any lawyer, but one who specializes in real estate and is up-to-date.

Whether your task will be relatively painless or a protracted ordeal depends largely on how accurately you price your property. That gets to your motive for selling it yourself. *Do you want to save the commission, or do you want to make some extra money by adding on a commission and keeping it?*

If the correct market price for your home is $100,000 and you decide you must have the full $100,000, your house would have to be priced with the 6% or 7% added on if you employed a broker. The price of $106,000 or $107,000 might be just enough extra to make it hard to sell. If you offer your house yourself at a net figure of $100,000, it might sell without too much effort. You will save the commission and get the full $100,000 without the $6,000 or $7,000 bite out of it.

If, however, your motive for handling it yourself is to get the $106,000 or $107,000, you would be not only saving the commission but earning an extra 6% or 7%.

Before you go for an inflated price, consider this: A markup of 6% or 7% is easily absorbed in a fat market like that of the late '70s, but it might be a real sale killer in the '80s. If it amounts to overpricing, you may still be sitting with that "For Sale" sign on your lawn three or four months later. At that point you will probably have to lower your price. Sometimes this strategy can cost more than just the lost three or four months. As mentioned earlier, there is such a thing as a property getting shopworn. Serious buyers get familiar with what is on the market in their targeted area, including how long it has been on the market. Once a house has been for sale five or six months, it will attract only sharpshooters who specialize in price-slashing offers. Thus, going for the high dollar could end in your taking the low dollar, especially if you have to capitulate by accepting a deal brought in by a broker.

GIVE YOURSELF ENOUGH LEAD TIME

Allow 90 days, at a minimum, to market your home. That's the *selling* time. You have to start earlier than that to get it ready for the market. The spectacle of the panicked seller sitting on an unsold home while he's supposed to be looking for a new home in a new city is not unfamiliar to brokers called in at a late hour. Any home, unless it is being offered in a boom market or below the market price, takes time to sell. Finding someone who wants to buy it is just the beginning. It might take days or weeks for him (or you) to find the financing.

Everything that was said in Chapter 15 about getting your home ready for sale goes double if you are going to sell it yourself. A glib agent can talk a client past a plaster crack or a piece of torn wallpaper, but it's much harder for the owner to do that. It may strike you as ironic to have to take time and spend money to fix something at the end of your occupancy that you have been putting up with for months or years, but you have to do it if you want to give yourself every break. It could mean the difference between landing a client and losing him to the open house down the street. If you doubt that anyone would turn down a house because of a little crack or some peeling wallpaper, you don't know the buying public. It might not happen in a brisk market, but in a slow market, buyers can take their pick, and they can get very picky. Maybe the buyer doesn't consciously reject a house because the kitchen needs painting. Maybe he just wanders into another property that is more appealing. What counts is that you have lost him.

MAINTAIN CONVENIENT HOURS

You must be available to show your home at all reasonable hours. You can decide that you will show it only by appointment, but you shouldn't be too rigid even about that. If you take an appointment-only stand, you're less likely to be bothered by the idle shopper who is unconcerned about your privacy, but then you might miss the earnest buyer who is running short of time and just happens into your neighborhood. Grabbing the impulse buyer is all the more important when you are selling your own home. When you have an agent, there's a possibility that such a buyer will be brought back. As an owner-seller, your first chance at him may be your only chance.

Keeping the property manned is another must. Some responsible, interested adult should be available most of the time. It is not enough to make your home accessible by having a painter, a baby-sitter or a child open the door. That's all right if an agent is coming to show it, but it's not good enough for the buying public. Most buyers have to be *shown* a home;

otherwise they race through without seeing it. If they are intent lookers, they need someone responsible there to answer their questions.

DON'T JUST SHOW IT—*SELL* IT!

Here's where your skills as a salesperson will be tested. Whether you pass the test depends on the thoroughness with which you prepare yourself.

Work up a professional-looking information sheet. How well do you know your property? Potential buyers will ask a lot of questions, and you'll have to respond. Be ready with the kind of information on the list at the end of this chapter. Nothing is more frustrating to both you and your customers than for you to have to look up the information every time it is needed.

Your fact sheet should be typed, but handwriting is okay if it is both large and legible. Have 100 copies photocopied. Customers are seldom prepared to take notes. Many times they are reluctant to appear that interested, but they will accept a printed fact sheet.

Take some color pictures of your house. Include the garden if it is unusual. (No people in the pictures, please.) Check with several photo finishers for a price on quantity reprints. You may not want to hand one out to every one who drops in, but at 15 or 20 cents per picture, photos are a terrific bargain in proportion to their effectiveness as a sales tool. Write the address of the property, the price, and your name and phone number on the back of each picture.

Photos and fact sheets will follow your customers home. Owners selling their own home are often puzzled by the fact that buyers who seem interested just disappear. Often a home gets crowded out of their consciousness by the sheer volume of new input. If you give a potential buyer a concrete reminder that looks more like something to file than to dispose of along with yesterday's classified section, you have a chance of keeping up with your competition.

Put up an attractive sign. Don't paint or tape over a used sign, particularly a sign with a real estate firm's name on it. That looks tacky, and no matter how you came into possession of the sign, it gives the appearance of being snitched property. You will create a much better impression for yourself as a businesslike seller and a better impression for your property if you put up a bright new sign in the front. Try to get a "For Sale by Owner" metal sign and a small add-on sign on which you can put your phone number. If you decide to hold your home open, you'll want an "Open" sign, too.

Signs are particularly effective sources of clients for both amateur sellers and real estate firms. A response to a sign is a much more valuable inquiry than a response to a newspaper ad. The sign caller is already in the neighborhood. His call means he approves of the area and he likes your house well enough to want to look inside. The caller on the classified ad is responding to general information only. He may or may not like your area or the external appearance of your home when and if he arrives.

Get ready for an invasion by real estate pros. From the hour that your first ad appears or you hang your "For Sale" sign, you will be besieged by calls and knocks on the door from real estate agents who want to list your house. If you have decided to try to sell your home yourself, you'll have to be clear and firm to counter their persuasive arguments.

You will cause endless confusion and complications for yourself if you tell agents that you want a certain price but they can keep anything above that as a commission if they find a buyer willing to pay more. Such a buyer may learn that you are offering a lower price and come to you directly, trying to cut the agent out. If you make that sale, you will be asking for a battle royal with that real estate firm. The firm could take you to court and prove it produced the client, and you would be liable for a commission no matter what price you took.

If you are disposed to try a half-and-half approach, set a time limit on your own brokering, exactly as you would with a professional broker. Give yourself 60 or 90 days or whatever time you choose. When the real estate agents start hounding you for a listing, you can tell them, "No listings until I've taken a fair crack at it myself." You will find it a much better procedure not to work in competition with agents. *Do your best and if you can't sell it, back off and let the agents take it.*

BRINGING THEM IN

The secret to finding the most able buyer in the shortest time is to generate a volume of traffic of selected buyers through your home.

If you know of someone who is a "natural" for your home, check out his interest before you put your home on the market. Any lead of this sort is worth following up, but it is not worth holding up other business for. Working with only one client at a time is a dangerous practice. There's too much that can go wrong—the buyer delays, changes his mind, can't obtain financing. On the contrary, you want to get as many buyers interested as you can.

If you shrink from waging that kind of campaign and your preferred strategy is to move from one hand-picked customer to another, it might take you forever to sell your home. If you feel strongly about doing it one at a time, it could mean you don't really have the stomach for playing broker, and maybe you should consider calling in a professional.

LOOKERS, BUYERS AND SELECTED CLIENTS

Some sellers err in the opposite direction. They've heard that you have to generate traffic to make a sale, so they are not happy unless they have a house full at all times. That can be as bad as not having enough.

If your home is in the $80,000 to $100,000 class, it will do you no good to have a parade of buyers in the $40,000 to $60,000 class. A common error for the amateur seller (it happens to professionals, too) is to sell himself hoarse to some earnest buyer who drinks in every word, only to learn that buyer can't carry half the payment on his home.

It's always tempting to become engaged with the visitor who expresses appreciation for your home. What you learn after a while is that most buyers love the property that's a notch or two beyond their buying reach.

So how do you weed out those buyers who for one reason or another won't be signing on the dotted line?

Always give the location at the opening of your ad. Location in general and small neighborhoods in particular are a powerful magnet. They are also an effective screen. If the ad reader wants to commute to a west-end job and you are on the far east side, it's better for both of you if you don't have to have a long telephone conversation to discover your mutual disinterest.

Location in this context can mean a subdivision name, a school district, an employment center or a geographic point from which an area derives its name, such as a city park, golf course or intersection of important thoroughfares. Check your professional competition—the real estate companies' ads. The way they designate your area is the way the public is most likely to be familiar with.

There is another advantage to mentioning location at the very beginning of your ad. It gets you the best location in the newspaper. Most newspapers list classified ads according to area. If yours is a large city, the city is broken into quadrants or major areas and the individual neighborhood listings are arranged alphabetically by location: Arcadia, Bentley, Chatham, Diamondpoint. If a buyer is interested in the Chatham district, he knows just where to look. If you start your ad without a geographic designation, it will land in the catch-all section at the end along with ads that begin "Cheap" or "Seller Desperate" and ads that begin with a price figure. Your ad will be lost there. Many readers, once they've reviewed the locations they are interested in, never get to the end of the listings.

Mention the price range in your ad. Some sellers have the idea that it is better not to scare possible buyers away by mentioning a price. The theory is that a buyer who is set on buying an $80,000 home will stretch for a $95,000 one if he falls in love with it. The truth is that buyers tend to stretch beyond their price range when they look. By failing to mention the price, you will be attracting dreamers who are hoping against hope that they can find something for nothing. You might even attract some who are looking for something more elaborate than your home. Either way, bringing in the wrong people is bad policy. It not only wastes time for both of you, it can also be disruptive. It's hard enough to split your attention when you have two qualified buyers at the same time. If you bring in the wrong ones, a right one can slip away while you are busy with the others.

You will keep away only the obviously disqualified if you mention the price. The stretch psychology isn't as valid as it was in a different market when interest rates were cheap. At today's costs, many buyers are finding they have to step down a price rung or two in order to qualify for a mortgage; stretching up is out of the question for them.

When you field calls from your ad, it is a good idea to restate your price and location for the callers before you let them come out. Typically, a buyer may be working from a list of 20 or 30 numbers he has copied from the ads. Sometimes, by the time he gets through to you, he has lost your ad. So make sure he knows what price and location you are discussing.

Think about your property in a new way. You may not have children in school or use public transportation, but nearby schools and bus routes could be two of the best features of your property. What about its proximity to offices, factories, colleges, recreational areas?

PROPERTY INFORMATION

Address:
Owner:
Telephone, home and business:
Cash price:
Seller financing available:
Price with seller financing:
Existing financing: balance, monthly payment, whether monthly payment includes taxes and insurance, annual taxes, name of mortgage holder, whether mortgage is assumable, whether it is a VA or FHA
Reason for selling:
Date of possession:

PHYSICAL DESCRIPTION

Size of lot:
Number of stories:
Architectural style:
Age:
Builder:
Basement (full, partial):
Number of bathrooms:
Number of bedrooms:
Master bedroom size:
Second bedroom size:
Third bedroom size:
Living room size:
Dining room size (separate or L):
Family room size:
Den size:
Utility room size:
Heating system type and age:
Water heater type and capacity:
Cooling system type:
Fireplace:
Energy efficiency: storm windows and doors, attic and wall insulation
Kitchen: dishwasher, disposer, built-in oven, washer, dryer, other appliances
Floors: wall-to-wall carpeting, hardwood, tile
Draperies: included or not
Roofing:
Siding:
Sewage, septic tank:
Garage or carport, number of cars:

Driveway, off-street parking:
Recent repairs, replacements:

LOCAL INFORMATION

Directions:
Schools: public or private, elementary and secondary
Shopping:
Public transportation:

20

Negotiating Your Way to a Contract

Strike a balance between give and take

Conflict between buyer and seller is inevitable, whether it is expressed or not. The buyer wants the most house for his money; the seller wants the most money for his house. The initial stages of bargaining can set the tone for the entire transaction. If you have an agent, you will be relying on him to direct events toward a mutually beneficial conclusion. If you are going it alone, you are in trickier waters.

ON YOUR OWN

The buyer walks through the property thinking, "I wonder whether they want to sell badly enough to cut the price?" The owner is concerned about making the best possible sale of his major investment, and often his pride in his home is involved.

The tension can be silent, masked by all the superficial courtesies that pass between people in a normal house-hunting encounter. If you are selling without an agent, you will need to draw out potential buyers and get them talking; otherwise, you could end up watching the back of buyer after buyer and never understand why.

For negotiations to proceed to the point where an offer can be made, both parties must be willing to ask for what they want and feel engaged enough to voice their objections and offer alternatives.

Initiate negotiations by seeking out areas of agreement. That doesn't mean getting a potential buyer to agree with you that your home is a well-built house in a superb location. The buyer doesn't want to be forced into flattery and will assume you are only trying to reinforce your price. Find out what attracted him to your property and build on that. Move on to issues that don't involve anybody's need to save face, such as the date of possession. Normally, that's not a touchy issue, though, like everything in a real estate sale, it can be.

You have a better chance of developing a conversation with a spirit of cooperation on the subject of possession than with other aspects of the contract. It's a good psychological step, too, because it gets the buyer thinking about actually moving in and makes the whole purchase seem more real to him.

Needless to say, price is the worst place to start. It is always a sensitive issue and the one most likely to arouse strong feelings.

You may be able to sense when a buyer is getting close to the contract-writing stage. When he comes back a number of times with advisers and friends in tow, you'll know he's serious. At this point sellers acting on their own behalf often make one of three mistakes:

• They don't sell. They just do a pleasant job of hosting and hope the buyer will voluntarily do the rest. That seldom happens.
• In their eagerness to hook the buyer and make a deal, they give away the store.
• They take such a tough bargaining stance that they drive the buyer away.

When you are working with a serious buyer, it's important for you to be objective about your property. Don't become defensive. Empathize enough with the buyer to reassure him. Be ready with all the information he needs and be confident and patient. Let him know that you want the negotiations to succeed. Be interested but don't appear hungry for a sale.

If you can't agree on one point, go on constructing the agreement in the areas in which you do see eye to eye. Don't close the door on any one point; just put the matter off until later.

If you recognize that you must compromise or give up on something you want, try to get everything else agreed on in writing. Then when you do back down on that point, the deal is essentially locked in. You have a contract and are on your way to closing.

USING AN AGENT

Most buyers and sellers find bargaining awkward and uncomfortable. An experienced agent can allay the fears of both parties and prevent many of the problems associated with face-to-face negotiations. Both buyers and sellers are likely to be more frank and open to reasonable compromise when they are talking to a third party.

Though you should employ the utmost tact in dealing directly with a buyer, you can be totally frank with your agent. The more so, the better. Agents know that sellers sometimes take positions they don't mean to defend to the very end, so let your agent know what is most important to you. Be as precise as possible about what is acceptable and what isn't. Your agent will be able to work far more efficiently for you if he is clear about what offers are going to be satisfactory to you.

If a cooperating agent brings in a serious buyer, arrange for him to talk with your agent before writing a contract. If that's not possible, ask him to get back to you before he goes into a contract session.

WHEN THE CONTRACT ARRIVES

Don't jump at the first contract. In fact, don't jump at any contract and unless you're very knowledgeable about real estate, never commit yourself without seeking a real estate attorney's advice. That doesn't mean you'll want to carry every offer to him, only those that pass your preliminary examinations.

As the seller you must make the final decision on the economic side of the offer. You know whether the price and terms give you what you must have. You, your agent and the lender have to evaluate the financial ability and sincerity of the buyer. Teamwork and cooperation are essential at this point. With your experts lined up, you must decide when and how to use them.

Money, people and the law are primary elements in any real estate sales contract. You need to be sure the parties to the contract are legally competent to do business with you. There must be mutual agreement as to the terms and conditions of the contract. The contract must be in writing and be freely offered by the buyer and accepted by the seller. Money or other valuable consideration must be exchanged for the title to the property.

The time you take to consider a contract is in itself an important strategy. The buyer may take weeks to make up his mind; once he does, either he or his agent is likely to pressure you for a quick decision.

Take the time you need to make an orderly evaluation. Otherwise, in your haste you may shortchange yourself or let a disadvantageous provision remain in force.

During that period, however, keep the buyer informed of your progress. Don't leave him hanging or he may have second thoughts or even panic. Remember, a buyer is legally free to withdraw his contract until it is accepted in writing by the seller.

Contracts often carry a time limit for the seller's consideration: "If not accepted by 5 p.m. on April 15, this contract is null and void." That's because buyers and their agents know that sellers sometimes use a contract to motivate a more indecisive buyer to top the offering with either a higher price or a bigger down payment. If you have good reason for not being able to meet the deadline, perhaps because your attorney or spouse is out of town, suggest another deadline that you could meet.

TAKE A HARD LOOK AT THE BUYERS

Analyze the buyers first. All the legal fine print in the world can't make a good deal with bad buyers. A judgment as to the sincerity of their intention to go through with the deal and their financial capability for doing so has to be made before considering any other part of the contract. Do they seem like knowledgeable buyers or is this the first house they've seen? Have they analyzed the house and terms carefully enough to make a considered judgement?

A buyer who knows the shortcomings of the house as well as the hurdles in getting financing and who still wants to go through with it is a better bet than one who may be derailed at the first negative comment from an inspector or a mortgage lender.

Find out as much as you can about the buyer and his financial background. If he is offering a sizable cash payment, is it his cash, or does he plan on borrowing it? If he plans on borrowing it, how likely is that? How do his employment prospects and salary look relative to the size of mortgage he is hoping to get? (See Chapter 17 if you will be helping the buyer with financing.)

No matter how good the deal looks on paper, if the buyer seems impulsive, frivolous, confused or irresponsible, the contract may not be worth much, no matter what it offers. Most veteran brokers have had the experience of holding what looks like a perfectly good contract only to discover the buyer has suddenly disappeared or taken a position in another city and has no intention of making good on the contract. (Such a contract expires simply by the purchaser's failure to satisfy any one of the contingencies.)

If you have acted as your own broker, you probably have a pretty clear impression of your buyers. If the contract was brought by an agent other than your own and your exposure to the buyers was brief, ask to have the selling agent come along for the contract presentation to fill you in.

THE CONTRACT ITSELF

The written bid for your house may take any number of forms, depending on where you live.

Contract to purchase, sales contract, binder receipt and option, agreement to buy and sell are all variations of the buyer's written offer for your property backed by an earnest money deposit.

One of the most useful bits of homework you can do to prepare yourself as a seller, whether you are using a broker or not, is to obtain blank copies of whatever forms of purchase offer are in widespread use in your area. If you study the forms or have your real estate attorney go over them with you, you can read through the legalese and concentrate on the elements of the deal itself.

Here's how to analyze an offer, piece by piece.

How substantial is the deposit? Before you spend any energy reacting to a contract, check out the deposit to determine whether it is a serious contract. Promises aren't worth much here. A large deposit backed by a promissory note to be redeemed a week or two hence doesn't have the same impact as a smaller amount of cash tendered right now.

What you want to know is this: How committed is the buyer? If he is taking little or no risk, it is well to conclude that he may be just fishing for a price reaction. In good times or bad, it's poor strategy to take your property off the market for an iffy buyer. It's more efficient to wash such a buyer out in the beginning and wait for a better deal than to try to hold a reluctant or weak buyer to his offer.

Even though a substantial deposit is a good start, it doesn't by itself guarantee a solid contract. There are other escape routes buyers provide themselves.

Is the offering price right? There is nothing in a contract that evokes such an emotional response from the seller as the price offered. *Try to keep an open mind on the price until you have studied the whole deal as a package.*

This is the time for you to be as objective as you possibly can. How realistic is your price? Was it based on an appraisal or a broker's competitive market analysis? How long was the house on the market before the first offer was presented? How many written offers have there been? What has happened in the market since you put your house up for sale? What do you and your broker know about the most recent sales of comparable properties? How much under their asking prices did they finally sell for?

It's a rare property that brings full price and the exact terms desired. Bargaining is to be expected. How much bargaining is a market fact you will have to determine at the precise time you are entertaining an offer.

Price by itself doesn't make or break the deal. Many times the amount of cash in the deal is more important than holding to the full price.

In the last analysis, it's how much the buyer wants the property and how much he is willing to give that determine whether it is a good deal for you. Does he want a price reduction, a soft down payment, a slow settlement, seller financing, and all sorts of guarantees besides? If you have to make a number of concessions (seller financing being a very large concession), you should hold to your price or near it.

Many a deal has been saved when the buyer and seller were within a few hundred or a thousand dollars on the price because the seller threw something extra in. The item may have real value, such as laundry equipment, or it may not be worth much but is nevertheless enough to let the buyer feel he saved face as a hard bargainer.

How much cash and whose is it? If the contract has an appealing lot of cash in it, make sure the buyer really has the cash. Don't accept vague answers. You have a right to know; after all, in exchange for his money, you're going to take your property off the market. If he is depending on selling another piece of real estate to raise the cash, that can be a major complication.

Beware of the contract that binds only you. Getting a seller to accept an offer that nails down the price and terms but leaves the buyer free to escape through a number of clauses is a favorite strategy of buyers. Contingency clauses vary in the degree of reasonableness.

Any contract contingency you accept should make it clear exactly what actions are expected of both parties and should have a cutoff date in it. As long as the contingencies are unsatisfied, you have a half-sold house: You are not free to sell it to someone else, but you don't have a firm buyer, either. The contract should require that the seller be informed in writing, and by the agreed-on time, that the buyer intends to act to void the contract and that otherwise the contract is in full force.

It is reasonable for a purchaser to want the protection of a clause that lets him out of the contract if he cannot obtain financing.

It is not reasonable for him to want to be let out of the contract if he cannot get financing that is several percentage points under the going rate. Nor is it reasonable for him to expect you to wait around while he shops every lender in the entire metropolitan area. A reasonable contingency clause on financing names an upper limit of what the buyer is willing to pay for a loan and a cut-off date after which the contract is voided.

It is also right and fair that the purchaser should have the opportunity to have your house independently appraised and evaluated for soundness of construction and state of repair. You should insist that the person or persons he is going to have examine the house be named in the contract by professional designation. Here the point goes to good faith. By insisting on such a designation, you find out whether the purchaser is really concerned about having an expert give him an opinion or just wants the right to veto the choice if he changes his mind.

Again, the time limit is very important. The sooner the contingencies in your contract are satisfied, the sooner you will know you have a sale.

There is no way you can anticipate in contract form all the things a buyer might do if he wants out of the contract, but by requiring prompt and written removal of the contingencies, you can close the most obvious loopholes.

Don't trade one uncertainty for another. Unless you have an easier sale in the works or good prospects of getting one, you may want to cooperate with the purchaser who must sell his house before he can buy yours. But bear in mind that puts you in the position of hinging the sale of a property you know on the sale of one you don't know. It can be a good deal in some circumstances, such as when a buyer falls in love with your home in the preliminary part of his house search before he has gotten organized to market his.

Before you enter into such an arrangement, however, you should seek the professional advice of a broker familiar with the area of your potential purchaser's house. You need to be assured that it is salable and reasonably priced. In any case, put a time limit in the contingency so that you are free to remarket yours before too much time has been lost.

Only accept this sort of contingency contract with carefully drawn safeguards. Your lawyer should review this. Ask for a hefty earnest money deposit. You can also try for a nonrefundable deposit should the deal fail.

Be careful what you guarantee. Occasionally, a purchaser asks a seller to guarantee that the roof won't leak, the heating system won't go out, or any number of other assurances.

If you do that, you are not making a sale, you are taking in a partner. If you guarantee the future, you will never be free. This is not a question of honesty; it is a question of reasonableness. There is no way you can promise that something in your home won't break down tomorrow. You should not undertake to remain responsible for your property once you have sold it. You are not a manufacturer, and it is, after all, used property.

If your lawyer agrees, your best counter may be to offer a contract clause in which you warrant there are no undisclosed material defects in the property.

21

Getting Ready for Settlement

It should go off without a hitch

Buyers often dread the day of closing because they are staring at such a huge outlay of cash, but as a seller you can look forward to collecting your bounty.

After all the commotion with agents, brokers and clients, finally the payoff is in sight. The time and the place of the settlement meeting have been set. The myriad details have been pulled together by the attorneys, title insurance or abstract company and lenders involved. (If you arranged for an escrow closing, most of this work will be done by mail and phone. See Chapter 12 for a discussion of settlement from the buyer's perspective.)

As the seller, you and your broker should be sure that everything necessary for a smooth closing is in the hands of the settlement attorney or closing officer as far in advance of settlement as possible.

Nothing makes a closing so tedious as having to sit around while the escrow officer telephones lenders, insurance companies, contractors and others for figures that should have been supplied before settlement. The result is that what could have been accomplished in 30 minutes takes a couple of hours.

There should be no arguing at the settlement table over who pays what because the contract and any escrow instructions should spell everything out.

If you are dealing with a broker, he normally provides you with a detailed cost sheet of what you can expect to net out of the settlement. In fact he should have given you a pretty close estimate at the time he presented the contract for signature.

If you are handling your own settlement, you can get an estimate within a few dollars at the time you arrange for closing, or "open escrow," whether it is with a title or abstract company or an abstract attorney.

Find out early who needs to be present at closing. Anyone named on the deed by which you hold title must sign the new deed by which you grant title. In many jurisdictions if you have married since you acquired title, your spouse will also have to sign the deed. If your co-owner is out of town, the escrow officer can send a deed to him or her to be signed before a notary public. This requires some advance planning to get the signed deed back in time for settlement.

Determine when you'll be paid. One thing you should inquire about before settlement is how long you will have to wait for your money. Your contract can require that the buyer pay in the form of a certified check, but don't expect to walk away from the settlement table with check in hand. Most settlement attorneys do not disburse checks until all the necessary documents have been recorded. An additional delay in disbursement can occur if the lender wants to review every detail of the settlement after it is over and then wait for the deed to be recorded before disbursing any funds.

If you are buying another property, it is convenient to have both settlements at the same office, scheduled back to back. That way, the timing of the disbursement is not a problem. You sign a paper authorizing the title company or attorney to assign the funds from your sale to your purchase.

THE PAPERS YOU'LL NEED

Here is a checklist of what will be needed to facilitate the closing:

• A copy of the sales contract and any documentation needed to show that contingencies have been removed or satisfied.
• All documents needed to complete the transfer of title. These are usually handled by the title insurance or abstract company and your attorney or closing officer. Depending on your situation, they may include certificate of title, deed, correcting affidavits, quitclaim deeds, survey and title insurance policy or binder. You'll want to be sure that the closing officer has the necessary papers showing that all judgments, liens and mortgages have been removed or satisfied.

Occasionally, private arrangements can come back to haunt you. Example: A member of the family lent you money to buy your home. The lender was businesslike enough to record the debt when it was made but not businesslike enough to release the lien when it was paid off. A similar problem can occur if a mechanic's lien has been filed against your property. Try to have all these matters resolved before settlement. Get professional advice as soon as they come to light and follow through until you are confident that the title is clear. (See Chapter 11, "Getting a Good Title.")

• Homeowners insurance policy. If the buyer plans to take over the unused portion of your hazard insurance, you'll need to make arrangements in advance so that all the paperwork will be ready on time.

• Prorations for ongoing expenses, such as insurance premiums, property taxes, accrued interest on assumed loans, and utilities (if not shut off between owners). The proration date is usually determined by local custom but can be different if the contract so specifies.

• Receipts showing payment of latest water, electric and gas bills.

• A certificate from your lender indicating the mortgage balance and date to which interest is paid. The closing officer usually obtains these figures calculated to the day of settlement.

YOUR SELLER COSTS

Look back at Chapter 12, where the buyer's settlement costs were discussed. Using the same set of assumptions, here is how the costs might break out for the seller. The purchaser paid $100,000 for the home. The contract calls for a $20,000 down payment and a 30-year $80,000 FHA mortgage at 12%. Settlement is January 2.

Commission to XYZ Realty	$7,000.00
Loan points (2½% of $80,000)	2,000.00
Appraisal fee	75.00
Lender's inspection fee	25.00
Closing fees	96.00
Document preparation fee	50.00
Title insurance policy (owner's portion)	524.00
Recording and transfer fees	13.50
Survey	50.00
Tax assessment for second half of previous year	480.00
Tax proration for January 1 and January 2 based on tax of $960	5.26
Total	$10,318.76

In addition to these closing costs the seller owes $65,885 on his mortgage, for a total of $76,203.76. He gets $100,000 from the buyer and nets $23,796.24 from the sale.

Once closing is over, you can walk away with a huge sense of relief and start getting ready for life in your new home.

GLOSSARY

Abstract of title

A written summary of the information in the public records affecting a title, including the chain of ownership and a record of liens or other encumbrances that could cloud the title's marketability.

Acceleration clause

A loan clause that allows the holder the right to demand the entire outstanding balance of the obligation to be due and payable at once when payment is in default.

Amortization

A method of liquidating a debt by making periodic payments of the principal and interest over a fixed period of time.

Assessment

The value that a taxing authority places on a property for real estate tax purposes. Also, a nonrecurring fee or special charge levied by public authority for a specific purpose and based on the value of the property.

Assumption

A method by which a buyer takes on the primary liability for the unpaid balance of an existing mortgage or deed of trust against the property. A legal assumption is different from purchasing the property "subject to" the existing loan without assuming personal liability for the mortgage debt.

Balloon payment

The unpaid principal amount of a loan or mortgage due on a specified date. This usually pays the loan in full.

Blanket mortgage

A single mortgage that covers more than one unit of property. The apartments in a cooperative building are covered by such a mortgage. May also be called a blanket trust deed.

Broker

An individual employed on a fee or commission basis to bring parties together and to assist in negotiating contracts between them. A real estate broker is licensed by the state to conduct a real estate business and to negotiate sales and purchases of property for a fee or commission.

Buy-down

Money paid to reduce the monthly mortgage payments of a buyer either during the entire term or for a shorter period. Buy-downs are frequently offered by builders.

Certificate of title

A written statement by an attorney or abstract or title insurance company indicating that the title to a piece of real estate is legally vested in the owner of record.

Chain of title

The history of the documents transferring title to a piece of real property. Each transfer by deed from one owner to another is called a link.

Chattel mortgage

A mortgage on personal property. Now called a security agreement.

Cloud on title

An outstanding lien, mortgage or encumbrance or a non-monetary claim, such as a right of first refusal to purchase the property, which, if valid, would affect or impair the title. A cloud on title can be removed by quitclaim deed, release or court action.

Commitment

A written agreement between a borrower and a lender in

which the lender promises to lend money at a future date under stated conditions.

Condominium

A form of ownership that provides a purchaser with title to a particular unit in a multiunit arrangement plus a proportionate interest in the land and common areas.

Conventional loan

A mortgage loan not guaranteed by VA or Farmers Home Administration or insured by FHA.

Conveyance

A written instrument, such as a deed, mortgage or lease, that is used to transfer an interest in real estate from one person to another.

Cooperative

A form of property holding in which a corporation that owns a building grants occupancy rights to participants, frequently through the use of a proprietary lease or shares in the corporation.

Deed

A written instrument that, if properly executed and delivered, conveys title to real property.

Deed of trust

Used in some states in place of a mortgage. The title is conveyed in trust to a third party, called a trustee, with the condition that the trustee will reconvey the title to the borrower when the debt is repaid. The trustee has the power to sell the land and pay the debt in the event of default.

Default

Failure to meet an obligation when due; especially failing to pay interest or principal on a mortgage when due. Also, nonperformance of mortgage covenants.

Due-on-sale

A clause in a mortgage that usually permits the holder to declare the entire obligation due and payable if the borrower sells or transfers the property. It can be used to prevent the assumption of the loan by another purchaser.

Easement

A right to make limited use of another person's land, such as a right of way or easement for gas lines.

Eminent domain

The right of a government to acquire private property for public or quasi-public use by condemnation; the owner must be compensated.

Encumbrance

Any valid claim that affects the fee simple title to property, such as mortgages, liens, easements or restrictions.

Equity

The interest or value an owner has in a property beyond any mortgage on it; the difference between fair market value and current indebtedness.

Escrow

The deposit of money and documents to the custody of a neutral third party until the terms and conditions of an agreement or contract are fulfilled. In some areas "going to escrow" refers to the procedure by which the sale and purchase of a home takes place.

Escrow account

A segregated trust account, used to hold funds pending the closing of a transaction.

Escrow agent

An organization or person having fiduciary responsibility to both the buyer and seller (or lender and borrower) to see that the terms of their agreement are carried out.

Exclusive listing

A written agreement that gives one real estate broker the right to sell a property for a specified period of time but not restricting the right of the owner to sell the property without payment of a commission.

Exclusive right to sell listing

A written agreement that gives a real estate agent the exclusive right to sell and entitles him to a commission regardless of who sells the property during the period of the agreement.

Fannie Mae (FNMA)

The Federal National Mortgage Association, a tax-paying corporation created by Congress to support the secondary mortgage market. It buys and sells mortgages originated by private lenders, whether they are FHA, VA or conventional loans.

Fee simple

The most comprehensive form of ownership or title to real estate, including the right to dispose of it and pass it to one's heirs.

FHA

The Federal Housing Administration, a government agency that insures the mortgages of qualified buyers against loss due to default, thus encouraging lenders to make mortgage loans on favorable terms.

Foreclosure

A procedure by which property pledged as security for a loan is sold or otherwise used to pay the defaulting borrower's debt.

Freddie Mac (FHLMC)

A quasi-governmental agency that purchases and pools conventional loans from savings and loan associations and banks. It sells insured participation sales certificates secured by these mortgage pools and Government National Mortgage Association bonds.

Grantee
The person who receives an interest in real property or a transfer of real property by deed; commonly the purchaser of a property.

Grantor
The person conveying an interest in real property; commonly the seller of a property.

Ground lease
An agreement that grants use of land only.

Hidden defect
A valid claim or encumbrance on a title not revealed in the public records; for example, forged instruments, unknown heirs or mental incompetency.

Homeowner's policy
A multiple peril insurance policy available for a premium to owners of private dwellings. Typically covers the home and its contents in case of damage or loss from fire, wind or theft and provides for personal liability coverage.

Interest
The fee charged for the privilege of borrowing money.

Joint note
A signed written agreement in which two or more parties acknowledge a debt and accept equal liability for repayment.

Joint tenancy
A form of equal ownership by two or more persons under which each co-owner's rights and interests pass directly to the surviving owners upon his or her death.

Land contract
A sales contract that lets the seller retain title to the property until the buyer has paid the full purchase price. Sometimes called a contract for deed.

Lease

A contract that gives a tenant possession and use of a property under the conditions and terms stated.

Lien

A legal hold or claim on the property of another as security for a debt or obligation; for example, mortgages, mechanics' liens or taxes.

Marketable title

A title with no defects or encumbrancs that would hinder an owner's ability to sell it.

Market value

The highest amount that a willing buyer would pay for a property and the lowest amount a willing seller would accept.

Mechanic's lien

A claim recorded against a property in order to secure priority of payment by one who has furnished labor or material but not been paid.

Mortgage

A formal document executed by an owner of property, pledging the property as security for payment of a debt or other obligation.

Mortgage banker

A lender who specializes in placing investors' funds in real estate loans. A mortgage banker usually continues to service the loans.

Mortgage broker

One who, for a fee, brings a borrower and a lender together.

Mortgagee

A lender in a transaction involving a mortgage instrument.

Mortgagor

A borrower or owner in a mortgage transaction who pledges property as security for a debt.

Mortgagee's title policy (lender's policy)
A title insurance policy that protects the lender against loss if the title proves imperfect.

Multiple listing service
A system that disseminates listing information to all of a group of member brokers and gives them the right to sell a property that has been exclusively listed with one of them, with the commission split between the broker who originally listed the property and the broker who sells it.

Negative amortization
A loan payment schedule under which the amount due increases rather than decreases because the amount of interest due exceeds the size of the monthly payment. The unpaid interest is added to the loan balance. Interest owed is then computed on the higher balance.

Open listing
A written agreement that gives a broker a nonexclusive right to sell a property, with only the broker who actually sells it being entitled to a commission.

Origination fee
A service charge made by a lender for the work in making a loan—preparation of papers, checking the credit of the borrower, inspecting, and sometimes appraising the property. Usually computed as a percentage of the face value of the loan.

Owner's title policy
A title insurance policy that protects the owner in the event of loss due to a defect in the title.

Perfecting title
The clearing of all claims against a title.

PITI
Principal, interest, taxes and insurance—the four elements that constitute the usual monthly mortgage payment.

Points

A one-time charge for making a loan, with each point equal to 1% of the loan principal. Loan discount points are charged by the lender at closing to increase the yield on a mortgage loan.

Prepayment penalty

A charge levied by a lender when a mortgage is paid off in part or in full prior to maturity. Mortgage agreements frequently limit the amount that can be prepaid in the early years of the loan or charge a penalty for prepayment.

Principal

The original sum of money owed; the amount on which the interest is calculated.

Purchase money mortgage

A mortgage given to the seller as part or all of the purchase price. The property serves as security for the loan.

Quitclaim deed

A deed relinquishing all interest, title or claim to a property by the grantor; it contains no covenants or warranties.

Realtor

A real estate broker who is a member of the National Association of Realtors.

Sales contract

An agreement between two or more parties, containing the terms and conditions of the sale. The contract usually must be written and signed by both parties.

Title

Evidence of ownership. In real estate, the document that contains all the facts on which proof of ownership is based. Title may be acquired through purchase, inheritance, devise, gift or foreclosure of a mortgage.

Title defect

Any legal right or interest in a property held by anyone other than the owner. Anything that adversely affects the owner's right to full ownership.

Title insurance

Insurance to protect owners and lenders against loss from defects in the title. (See "Mortgagee's title policy" and "Owner's title policy.")

Title search

The examination of all public records to disclose all facts pertinent to the title of the property.

Title search fee

The charge for the examination (and unrelated to the premium for title insurance).

Trust deed

A deed given to a trustee by a borrower granting legal title to the trustee until the loan is fully repaid to the lender.

Trustee

The person who holds title to property for the benefit of another or until the performance of an obligation.

Trustor

The person who deeds property to a trustee to be held as security until he has met his obligation to a lender under the terms of a trust deed.

VA

The Veterans Administration, a government agency that protects lenders against loss by guaranteeing loans made to qualified veterans through its home loan guaranty program.

Vendee

The buyer of real or personal property.

Vendor

The seller of real or personal property.

INDEX

A

Abstract of title, defined, 279

Abstract plus attorney's opinion, 149

Acceleration clause, defined, 279

Adjustable-rate mortgage (ARM)
also known as AML, 36
effect on prices, 23
elements of, 31-32
questions to ask about, 33
sample amortization of, 54 table
sample rate and payment adjustments, 56-57 table
types of, 35-38

Adjusted sales price, 193

Advertising
classified, 83-90
by owner seller, 255-59

Advisers, professional
appraisers, 109, 131-34, 139, 222-24
attorney, 131, 141-42, 263-65, 271

buyer-agent, 124-26
fees for, 131
home inspector, 134-35
need for, in buying, 129-32

Affordability
how to determine, 17-19
worksheet for monthly payments, 18-19

Agent, 28. *See also* Buyer-agent
commission for, 124
compared with real estate counselor, 8-9
defined, 120
how to find, 122-24
relationship to buyer, 124
relationship to seller, 122
as salesperson, 72-73
services of, to seller, 244-45
skills required of, 126

Alabama, 148

Alaska, 148, 224, 233

American Home Shield, 135

American Institute of Real Estate Appraisers, 133

American Land Title
   Association, sample
   policy of, 160-69
American Society of
   Home Inspectors, 134
AML. *See* Adjustable-rate
   mortgage
Amortization
   amortization table, 23
   defined, 279
Amortization, negative,
   33, 37-38
   and adjustable-rate
      loans, 33
   defined, 286
   and payment cap, 34
Appraisal
   as bargaining tool, 132,
      139
   for buyer, 131-34
   for condominium, 224
   cost of, 133
   for owner-seller, 219,
      222-24
   form of, 133
   structural and
      mechanical, 134-35
Appraisers, 131-34, 222-24
   address of American
      Institute of Real
      Estate Appraisers,
      133
   address of Society of
      Real Estate
      Appraisers, 133
Arizona, 148, 149, 157
ARM. *See* Adjustable-rate
   mortgage
Assessment, defined, 279
   tax angles of, 187

Assets, for determining
   net worth, 14-15
Assumability
   of adjustable-rate
      mortgages, 35
   of existing loans, 46-49,
      52
   of fixed-rate mortgage,
      30
   of refinance-blend
      mortgage, 39
   of seller-financed loan,
      228
   of wraparound
      financing, 50-51
Assumption, 47-49
   defined, 279
   unauthorized, 48
Attorney's record search
   and opinion, 149

B

Balloon mortgage, 45
Balloon payment, 49, 185,
   228
   defined, 279
Bank, commercial
   for mobile home loans,
      105
   as mortgage lenders, 24,
      26-27
Bargaining. *See*
   Negotiation
Basis, 191
   defined, 181
   effect of settlement
      costs on, 183-84
   record-keeping for,
      182-84

relationship to taxable
    profit, 181-84
and zero percent
    financing, 186
Binder. *See* Contract
Blanket mortgage,
    defined, 280
Blended rate, 48, 50-52
Broker, 28, 212-13
    commissions of, 67, 124
    defined, 120, 280
    how to choose, 127-28,
        235-40
    obligation to seller, 67
    reputation of company
        of, 236-38
    services performed by,
        127-28, 244-45
Builder
    and Home Owners
        Warranty, 135-36
    other warranty
        programs of, 136
    and zero interest plan,
        45
Buy-down loans. *See*
    Permanent buy-down;
    Temporary buy-down
    defined, 280
Buyer
    analysis of, by owner-
        seller, 265-66
    needs of, 68-69
    as negotiator, 140
    net worth of, 14-16
    preoccupations of, 65-68
    and prequalifying
        interview, 22-23
    psychology of, 146
    relation to agent, 124

strategy, 65-66
Buyer-agent, 124-26
Buying. *See also*
    Homeownership; House-
    hunting
    goals, 3-9
    needs versus wants,
        68-75
    strategy for, 64-90
    tax implications of,
        179-84
Buy versus rent debate, 6

C

California, 148, 157, 219
Caprice value of real
    estate, 108-09
Cash, amount needed to
    buy, 13-15
Cash-flow tie-up, as
    homeownership burden,
    11
Certificate of reasonable
    value, 134, 224
Certificate of title,
    defined, 280. *See also*
    Title, defined
Chain of title, defined, 280
Chattel mortgage, defined,
    280
Checklist
    for house-hunting, 70-71
    for mortgage
        comparison, 61-63
    of property information
        for buyer, 257-59
    for seller's house
        inspection, 213-17

for settlement costs,
176-77

Classified advertising
elements of good,
255-57
how to read, 83-90
in house hunting,
83-90

Closing. *See* Settlement

Cloud on title, defined,
280

Colorado, 149

Commercial bank. *See*
Bank, commercial

Commission
for agent, 8
payment of, to broker,
67, 243

Commitment, defined,
280-81

Commuting, as housing
cost, 92-94

Conditional commitment,
133, 224

Condominium
advantages of, 99-101
defined, 99, 281
disadvantages of, 101-03
lower cost of, 94

Connecticut, 148

Contingency clauses,
141-42, 269-271

Contract
as binding agreement,
141
breach of, 53
clauses in, 143
earnest money deposit,
142-44, 267
elements of, 141-47,
213, 264

how to analyze, as offer,
263-71
owner-seller negotiation
of, 260-71
provision for credit
check in, 229-31
time limit on, 145-46,
264-65

Contract for deed. *See*
Contract sale

Contract sale, 49-50

Conventional loan,
defined, 281

Conveyance, defined, 281

Cooperative, defined, 281

Cost of settlement, 171-74,
276

Creative financing, 24, 27,
46-53
seller considerations of,
226-29
tax angles of, 186

Credit. *See also* Lender;
Loan
check by seller-lender,
229-31
what lender looks for,
20-21

Credit reporting agency,
20, 229

D

Deductions. *See* Tax
benefits

Deed, defined, 281

Deed of trust, defined, 281

Default, defined, 281

Deposit, 142- 44, 267

Deregulation
effect on mortgages, 27

Down payment
    ban on borrowing of, 17
    for conventional loan,
        14
    for FHA loan, 13
    for mobile home, 104
    for VA loan, 13
    size of, 144-46
Due-on-sale clause, 48-50
    defined, 282
    in fixed-rate mortgage,
        30

E

Earnest money. *See*
    Contract
Easement, defined, 282
Eminent domain, defined,
    282
Encumbrance, defined,
    282
Energy credit, for
    homeowners, 189-90
Equity. *See also* Shared-
    equity mortgage;
    Growing-equity
    mortgage
    defined, 282
Equity loan, 205-06
Escrow, defined, 171, 282
Escrow account, defined,
    282
Escrow officer, 28, 52, 171
    defined, 282
Exclusive listing, 242
    defined, 283
Exclusive right to sell
    listing, 241-42
    defined, 283

F

Fannie Mae. *See* Federal
    National Mortgage
    Association
Federal Home Loan Bank
    Board, 36
Federal Housing
    Administration
    (FHA), 13, 31, 35, 41,
    47, 52, 105, 133, 134,
    172, 173, 175, 223
    defined, 283
Federal National
    Mortgage
    Association, 40, 133,
    172, 233-34
    defined, 283
Fee simple, defined, 283
FHA. *See* Federal
    Housing
    Administration
Financing
    lenders, 22-28
    for mobile home,
        104-05
    related to property
        location, 224
    by seller, 46-53, 226-34
    types of, 29-63
Financing sources. *See*
    Lenders
Fixed-rate mortgage,
    29-30
    sample monthly
        payments of, 59
    table
Fixed-rate mortgage with
    call option, 44-45
Florida, 148
FNMA. *See* Federal

National Mortgage
Association
Foreclosure, 228
defined, 283
Freddie Mac, defined,
283-84

Growing equity mortgage
(GEM), 43-44
compared with fixed-
rate and graduated-
payment mortgages,
58 table

G

GEM. *See* Growing-equity
mortgage
Georgia, 149
Glossary, 277-88
GNMA. *See* Government
National Mortgage
Association
Government National
Mortgage
Association, 172
GPAML. *See* Graduated-
payment mortgage
with adjustable-rate
feature
GPARM. *See* Graduated
payment mortgage
with adjustable-rate
feature
GPM. *See* Graduated-
payment mortgage
Graduated-payment
mortgage (GPM),
30-31
sample amortization of,
55 table
Graduated-payment
mortgage with
adjustable-rate
feature, 37-38
Grantee, defined, 284
Grantor, defined, 284
Ground lease, defined, 284

H

Hawaii, 148, 224, 233
Hidden defect, defined,
284
Home improvement, effect
on taxes of, 187-89
Homeowner policy, 275
defined, 284
Homeownership
benefits of, 10
disadvantages of, 3, 5-6,
11
as enforced savings
program, 3, 10
tax angles of, 3, 178-99
Home Owners Warranty,
coverage under,
135-36
House-hunting. *See also*
Buying
checklist for, 70-71
and personal prejudices,
81-83
Housing
advantages and
disadvantages of new,
95-97
advantages and
disadvantages of old,
97-99
condominium, 99-103
hidden costs in, 92-95
mobile home, 103-05

HOW. *See* Home Owners Warranty
HUD. *See* U.S. Department of Housing and Urban Development

I

Idaho, 148, 158
Illinois, 148
Index for mortgage payment changes, 33-35
 for ARM or AML, 35-37
Indiana, 148
Inspection
 professional, 134-35
 time for, 146-47
 your own, 213-17
Installment sale. *See* Contract sale
Insurance on seller-financed mortgages, 231-32
Insurance, title, 148-52
 defined, 288
 and future marketability, 150
 how to buy, 150-52
 for lender, 150-51
 for owner, 151-52
 sample policy of, 160-69
 states issuing, 148-49
Interest, defined, 284
Interest rates
 cap on, in adjustable-rate mortgage, 32-35
 and refinance-blend mortgage, 38-39
 and refinancing, 30

Internal Revenue Service, 45, 154, 180, 184-86, 188, 191
Iowa, 149, 150

J

Joint note
 defined, 284
Joint tenancy, 157, 158
 defined, 284

K

Kansas, 148
Kentucky, 149

L

Land contract, 49-50
 defined, 284
Lease, defined, 285
Lease with option to buy, 52-53
Lease-purchase, 53
Lenders, 22-28
 commercial bank, 24, 26-27, 105
 mortgage company, 24, 27-28
 owner-seller, 24, 46-53, 226-34
 and prequalifying interview, 22-23
 savings and loan, 24, 25-27, 105
Liabilities, for determining net worth, 15
Lien, defined, 285
 and title problems, 151

Listing
  kinds of, 240-43
  multiple, 52, 244-45
Listing agreement
  elements of, 243
  exclusive, 242
  exclusive right to sell,
    241-42
  nonexclusive, 242
  oral, 242-43
Loans. *See also*
    Mortgage; Lender;
    Financing
  adjustable-rate, 23,
    31-38
  balloon, 45
  blended-rate, 39
  checklist for
    comparison, 61-63
  costs of, 25-26
  equity, 205-06
  fixed-rate, 29-30
  fixed-rate with call
    option, 44-45
  government-backed, 17,
    35, 41, 47, 52, 105,
    172
  graduated-payment,
    30-31
  growing-equity, 43-44
  insurance on seller-
    financed, 231-32
  permanent buy-down,
    40-41
  and points, 25-26, 173
  shared-appreciation,
    41-42
  shared-equity, 42-43
  temporary buy-down, 41
  zero interest plan, 45-46
Location. *See also*

Neighborhood
  and caprice value,
    108-09
  importance of, 68-69,
    106-19
  and resale value, 107
Louisiana, 149, 158

M

Maine, 149
Manufactured home. *See*
    Mobile home
Market analysis, 132, 245
Marketable title, defined,
    285
Market value, defined, 285
  versus appraised value,
    223
Maryland, 148
Massachusetts, 149
Mechanic's lien, defined,
    285
Michigan, 148
Minnesota, 149
Mississippi, 149
Missouri, 148
Mobile home, 103-05
Montana, 148
Monthly payment,
    worksheet for
    determining, 18-19
Mortgage. *See also*
    Lender; Loan
  adjustable-rate, 31-38
  adjustable-rate with cap,
    36-37
  adjustable-rate without
    cap, 35-36
  balloon, 45

checklist for
comparison, 61-63
defined, 285
fixed-rate, 22, 29-30
fixed-rate with call
option, 44-45
graduated-payment,
30-31
graduated-payment with
adjustable-rate
feature, 37-38
growing-equity, 43-44
ideal adjustable-rate,
34-35
permanent buy-down,
40-41
refinance-blend, 38-40
shared-appreciation,
41-42
shared-equity, 42-43
temporary buy-down, 41
types of, 29-63
zero interest plan, 45-46
Mortgage banker, defined,
285
Mortgage broker, defined,
285
Mortgage company, as
loan source, 24, 27-28
Mortgage Guaranty
Insurance Corp., 231
Mortgage market,
secondary, 233-34
Mortgage payment. See
also Down payment;
Monthly payment
acceleration of, in
adjustable-rate, 33
adjustment of, in
adjustable-rate with
cap, 37

balloon payment loan,
11
index determining
changes in, 33
tax deductibility of,
179-81
worksheet for
determining, 18-19
Mortgagee, defined, 285
Mortgagee's title policy,
defined, 286
Mortgagor, defined, 285
Moving expenses, 197-99
Multiple listing service,
52, 244-45
defined, 286

N

National Association of
Real Estate Brokers,
121
National Association of
Realtors, 121
Negotiation
broker role in, 127-28,
263
of contract by owner-
seller, 260-62
initiated by buyer, 140
items subject to, 141
psychology of, 139-40,
260-62
in settlement, 175
strategy of, 138-47
use of appraisal in, 132,
139-40
Neighborhood. See also
Location
appraisal of future,
112-13

boundaries of, for
property value,
109-10
effect of public
decisions on, 116-19
housing compatibility
within, 111
negative factors of,
113-15
restoration trend in,
115-16
Net worth
of buyer, 14-16, 230
worksheet for figuring,
15-16
Nevada, 148, 158
New Hampshire, 149
New Jersey, 148
New Mexico, 149, 158
New York, 148
Nonexclusive listing, 242
North Carolina, 148
North Dakota, 149

O

Ohio, 148
Oklahoma, 149
$125,000 exclusion, 195-96
Open listing, defined, 286
Oral listing, 242-43
Oregon, 148
Origination fee, 173-74,
182-83
defined, 286
Over-55 exclusion, 195-96
Owner-seller
advertising by, 252
analyzing contract,
263-65
negotiation by, 260-62

resources needed,
247-49
selling strategy for,
209-17, 251-59
and settlement, 273-76
as source for mortgage
funds, 24, 46-53,
226-34
time required to sell,
249-50
Ownership. See
Homeownership
Ownership, joint, 157
Owner's title insurance
policy, defined, 286

P

Partnership, 158-59
in shared-equity
mortgage, 42-43
Payments. See Mortgage
payments
Pennsylvania, 148, 149
Perfecting title, defined,
286
Permanent buy-down
loan, 40-41
PITI, defined, 286
PMI Private Mortgage
Insurance, 231
Points, 173-74, 182-83. See
also Origination fee
defined, 287
and loans, 25-26, 276
Prepayment penalty, 30,
191
defined, 287
of refinance-blend
mortgage, 39

Prequalifying for loan,
22-23
President's Commission
on Housing, 103
Price
in buying strategy, 66-67
setting by seller, 218-25
Principal, defined, 287
Profit, 191
rollover of, 192
Property
choosing among types
of, 91-105
importance of location,
69
Purchase money
mortgage, defined,
287
Purchase offer. See
Contract

Q

Qualifications for buyer,
13-21
Quitclaim deed, defined,
287

R

Real estate agent. See
Agent
Real estate prices. See
Price
Real Estate Settlement
Procedures Act, 172
Realtist, 121
Realtor, 120-21
defined, 287
Realtor associate, 121
Record-keeping, 182-84

Refinance-blend mortgage,
38-40
Refinancing
of adjustable-rate loans,
33
and interest rates, 30
penalty for, 35
of refinance-blend
mortgage, 39
Remodeling versus selling,
204
Rental, long-range trend
in, 7
Resale value, and
property location, 107
RESPA. See Real Estate
Settlement
Procedures Act
Rhode Island, 148-49

S

Sale, tax consequences of,
191-97
Sales contract, defined,
287
Sales tricks, 211-12,
251-53
SAM. See Shared-
appreciation mortgage
Savings and loans, 24, 27,
35, 40, 43, 105
Second mortgage, 46-47,
227
Fannie Mae
requirements on,
233-34
insurance for, 232
Seller financing,
and buyer credit check,
229-31

contract sale, 49-50
direct assumption of
    existing loan, 47-49
effect on owner-seller
    pricing, 224-25
lease with option to buy,
    52-53
lease-purchase, 53
and market for paper,
    232-34
risks of, 231
tax implications of,
    196-97
wraparound, 50-52
Selling
    alternatives to, 203-08
    assessing buyer net
        worth, 230-31
    home inspection
        checklist, 213-17
    and home presentation,
        209-12, 251-53
    pricing of home, 218-25
    tax implications of,
        191-97
SEM. *See* Shared-equity
    mortgage
Settlement
    also known as escrow,
        171
    costs of, 171-74, 276
    defined, 171
    effect of local custom
        on, 173
    negotiation in, 175
    owner-seller planning
        of, 273-75
    tax deduction of
        expenses, 182-84
    worksheet of costs,
        176-77

Settlement Costs and You,
    172
Settlement officer
    abstract company, 170
    attorney, 170, 272
    need for, 170-71
    title company, 170
Shared-appreciation
    mortgage, 41-42
    tax angles of, 186
Shared-equity mortgage,
    42-43
Society of Real Estate
    Appraisers, 133
South Carolina, 149
South Dakota, 149

T

Tax
    adjustment of
        withholding, 181
    and basis, 181-84
    and homeownership,
        185-90
    on profit, 191-97
Tax benefits. *See also* Tax
    deferment
    energy credit, 189-90
    in early years, 180
    of mortgage payments,
        179-81
    moving expenses,
        197-99
    points, 182-83
    prepaid interest, 183
    property tax
        adjustments, 183
    property taxes, 180

of settlement expenses,
182-84
Tax deferment
effect of adjusted sales
price, 193
as homeownership
benefit, 10
on profit, 193
restrictions on, 195
rollover, 192
Tax forms
1040X, 194
2119, 193, 194
Tax shelter, $125,000
exclusion, 195-96
Temporary buy-down, 41
Tenancy in common, 158
Tenancy by entirety, 157
Tennessee, 149
Texas, 122, 149, 150, 158
Ticor Home Protection,
135
Ticor Mortgage Insurance,
231
Title. *See also* Abstract
plus attorney's
opinion; Attorney's
record search and
opinion
common problems with,
153-56
dangers of cloudy, 152
defined, 148, 287
forms of, 149-50
how to avoid problems
with, 156-57
insurance on, 148-52
how to take, 157-59
for married couples,
157-58
search, 288

for unmarried people
buying together,
158-59
Title closing. *See*
Settlement
Title defect, defined, 288
Title insurance. *See*
Insurance, title
Title search, defined, 288
Title search fee, defined,
288
Treasury securities, as
index, 35, 36, 37
Trust deed, defined, 288
Trustee, defined, 288
Trustor, defined, 288

U

Uniform Settlement
Statement, 172-73
U.S. Department of
Housing and Urban
Development, 104,
172
Utah, 149

V

VA. *See* Veterans
Administration
Vendee, defined, 288
Vendor, defined, 288
Vermont, 149
Veterans Administration,
13, 31, 35, 41, 47, 52,
105, 133, 134, 172,
173, 223-24, 288
Virginia, 149

W

Warranty, new home. *See*
  Home Owners
  Warranty
Warranty, used home
  American Home Shield,
    135
  Ticor Home Protection,
    135
Washington, 149, 158
West Virginia, 149
Wisconsin, 149
Worksheet
  for determining ability
  to make monthly
    mortgage payment,
    18-19
  for figuring net worth,
    15-16
Wraparound mortgage,
  51-52
Wyoming, 149

Z

Zero interest plan (ZIP),
  45-46
  tax angles of, 185-86